D0811986

# Columbia University

# Contributions to Education

## Teachers College Series

# No. 18

# AMS PRESS
## NEW YORK

# SYSTEMATIC STUDY IN THE ELEMENTARY SCHOOLS

BY

Lida Belle Earhart, Ph. D.

Instructor in Elementary Education, Teachers College,
Columbia University

Published by

TEACHERS COLLEGE, COLUMBIA UNIVERSITY

NEW YORK CITY

1908

**Library of Congress Cataloging in Publication Data**

Earhart, Lida Belle, 1864-
    Systematic study in the elementary schools.

    Reprint of the 1908 ed., issued in series: Columbia
University contributions to education. Teachers college
series, no. 18.
    Originally presented as the author's thesis, Columbia.
    Includes bibliographical references.
    1. Study, Method of. I. Title. II. Series:
Columbia University. Teachers College. Contributions
to education, no. 18.
LB1049.E2  1972        372.1'3'02814        73-176739
ISBN 0-404-55018-5

Reprinted by Special Arrangement with Teachers
College Press, New York, New York

From the edition of 1908, New York
First AMS edition published in 1972
Manufactured in the United States

AMS PRESS, INC.
NEW YORK, N.Y.    10003

# TABLE OF CONTENTS

## CHAPTER V

### Are Pupils Being Taught to Study Systematically in the Elementary Schools

## CHAPTER VI

### Can Pupils in the Elementary School be Taught to Study Systematically

# CHAPTER I

## THE NATURE OF LOGICAL STUDY

*One important phase of a teacher's work.*

Not the lightest of the duties required of children in school is the preparation of lessons from day to day through a series of years. Since not only the product but also the process of studying is of value to pupils who are preparing for life in an environment which furnishes frequent occasion for the use of both, it is an important part of the teacher's mission to see that the children know how to prepare their lessons intelligently and systematically.

*The necessity of knowing the logical and psychological basis of the process of studying.*

Should teachers desire to give their pupils training in correct habits of studying, they must possess a knowledge of the *logical* and *psychological* basis of the studying process in order to be scientific in their procedure. It might be added that their interest and their enthusiasm in the cause also depend upon this knowledge, since a subject which is not well understood, or which is misunderstood, is not likely to arouse an attitude of enthusiasm toward itself, or intelligent zeal in its application.

The question then is pertinent, what are the logical and also the psychological bases for the process of studying?

*Meaning of study.*

Before answering this question, a definition of the term studying is necessary in order that misunderstanding may be avoided. Studying in its highest sense is the process of assimilating knowledge, of reorganizing experience. As ordinarily employed, the term studying often means much less than this, and includes any mental activity directed towards the accomplishment of some end, whether that end be the memorizing of facts in a geography lesson, the learning of a story in reading, or the mastering of a list of words in spelling. In this common usage of the word it includes the mind's activity that is directed towards the acquisition of ideas, whether these ideas become an organic part of knowledge or not. Learning dates in history, and committing poems and definitions to memory do not always involve the assimilation of knowledge, yet teachers call the effort to accomplish these tasks by the same name that is applied to the mental efforts of a philosopher who is engaged upon some weighty problem. The two kinds of studying are quite different. The one is more mechanical than the other and results largely in accretion of facts. The other is organic and results in rearrangement and assimilation of ideas: in short, it involves thinking. It is this latter form of mental activity, which is generally acknowledged to be of a higher type than the first, that is the object of investigation and discussion in this paper. While any form of studying might be called psychological, because it involves the employment of mental processes, only that form of studying can be called logical which involves a thought-situation or problem, and thinking which is influenced by the nature of such a situation.

*The kind of thinking employed in studying.*

The thinking which is employed in studying is reflective or purposive thinking as distinguished from spontaneous thinking. In the latter sort, the ideas are not controlled by the thinker. They come and go at random. But in reflective or purposive thinking, there is a definite end in view and the ideas are selected and controlled so as to accomplish this end. When a person gives the rein to fancy and lets his thoughts wander where they will, his thinking is of the spontaneous kind; but when he sets himself to accomplish some task, to solve a problem, or to find the way out of some difficulty, he controls his thoughts and chooses or rejects the ideas which come into consciousness, taking as the basis of his choice the bearing which these ideas have upon the end he is trying to reach.

*The origin of the incentive to thought—the problem.*

But back of the process of reflective thinking lies the determination of the problem or purpose which causes the thought and governs its course. In this determination of the problem lies the logical basis of study, hence it is important to know whence this problem is derived and by whom it must be felt as a problem if it is to influence thought. If we search our own minds to find out what it is in our everyday life which sets us to thinking, we find that it is some break in the even course of our experience which requires adjustment. Facts thrust themselves upon us in books, or apart from them, and we do not at once see their relation to our previous knowledge. Emergencies arise in which our habitual ways of doing things fail us and yet activity of some sort is desirable, or, it may be, imperative. We find ourselves lacking in the knowledge needed to direct our actions or to explain a situation which has presented itself; or we find discrepancies existing among ideas, and feel it necessary to bring about some reconciliation. It may be that our faith in the validity of our own knowledge is shaken and we are at a loss to know what to believe. Needs of all sorts press upon us, from those which are most primitive to those which are the result of education and experience. Some of these needs function at the present time and demand immediate attention. Others belong to the future, but require effort now in order that they may be met when they arise. These needs are a part of experience both in school and in life aside from school, and whenever they are sufficiently imperative they give rise to thought or study.

Again, tension in experience may arise because of lack of power to apply knowledge already possessed. This lack may be due to a need of insight into the relations existing between our knowledge and the concrete instance involving its use. This of itself is a thought-situation and an occasion for study. Or, the lack of power may be due to lack of skill; it demands concentration of attention and repetition of some process, rather than the exercise of the higher mental activities in order to meet the situation, though thinking is involved in determining the cause of the difficulty, in selecting the means to overcome it, and in judging of the efficiency of the latter when they are employed. In both of these cases, therefore, real study is necessary.

The aim of thought is to readjust experience so that tension or friction shall disappear and harmony prevail. Each specific situation presents its own peculiar incentive to thought and furnishes the occasion for its exercise. It is clear that the thinking thus occasioned cannot be of the spontaneous kind but must be reflective, purposive in its nature. Its course, too, is not complete until the validity of its results has been tested in some way. Conclusions and theories must be tried by further experience before their validity can be affirmed positively. When, however, their use has become habitual so that they have reached the mechanical stage of application, they present no further aim to thought, and the problem is regarded as solved; i. e. the " studying " is completed.

### Thinking, memorizing, and habit-forming.

In this connection, the relation between thinking and memorizing, and thinking and habit-formation should be noted. In thinking, ideas are associated according to their meaning, and when the process is ended, memorizing is at least partially accomplished, and that, too, in its best form. Reviewing the associations thus established completes the process. This is rational memorizing as distinguished from that which is purely mechanical. In habit-forming, thinking may be very prominent during the first stages. The form of activity to be learned, the way of responding to a certain situation must sometimes be chosen as the result of reflection, and progress in efficiency must be watched with care until the mind is freed from conscious oversight of the process.

### Relation of the problem to the person who is to study.

It is self-evident that in normal conditions the tension, the lack of harmony, or want of completeness must be within the experience of the person or persons who are to do the thinking, since the thinking arises from personal motives. A thing is of interest and worth doing, and demands to be done because in some way it affects our own welfare and the equilibrium of our ideas. Professor James, in discussing interest, says: " You will understand this abstract statement easily if I take the most frequent of concrete examples—the interest which things borrow from their connection with our own personal welfare. The most natively interesting object to a man is his own personal self and its fortunes. We accordingly see that the moment a thing becomes connected with the fortunes of the self, it forthwith becomes an interesting thing. Lend the child his books, pencils, and other apparatus: then give them to him, make them his own, and notice the new light with which they instantly shine in his eyes. He takes a new kind of care of them altogether. In natural life all the drudgery of a man's business or profession, intolerable in itself, is shot through with engrossing significance because he knows it to be associated with his personal fortunes."[1] If the problem is to have interest, and is to be a motive power to the child, it must grow out of his own experience, some situation in relation to himself, otherwise no genuine thinking will result.

For a teacher in the elementary schools to assign a lesson without first preparing the class so that the pupils go to their work with a definite problem in view, and that problem one which touches them vitally, one which they have some interest in accomplishing, is to invite mechanical memorizing, and that, as has been said, is not study in the higher sense because it is not the assimilation of knowledge. When the teacher gives the problem to the class, which is usually the case when there is any aim present at all, the pupils may have a motive for thoughtful work and they may not. It depends upon the extent to which they recognize the problem as valid for them, as involving their own needs, as possessing personal interest, as presenting a situation which they accept as theirs. Thoughtful study will depend upon their appropriation of the problem as given by the teacher. But if the teacher can so direct the experience of her pupils that this problem arises in their own consciousness of need, then it is felt to be theirs and the situation is most favorable for thinking.

*Need of definiteness of aim.*

Another point of importance to note in regard to the problem is the fact that it should be as clearly defined as possible before its solution is undertaken. To be aware that there is a crisis or tension in experience is one thing; to have analyzed the situation so as to see just where the difficulties lie is quite another; and to determine possible modes of accomplishing the solution is still another. It is as if a person, who has seen a long pendulum set swinging in a north-and-south direction, discovers after several hours that the record shows a change in direction, and being

---

[1] James. Talks to Teachers, pp. 94-95.

puzzled, should ask, not " Why does it swing?" because he saw it set in motion; but " Why, having been started to swing in one direction, does it now swing in another?" Probably several answers suggest themselves, some to be rejected at once as manifestly contrary to fact and consequently impossible. Only those hypotheses are accepted tentatively for investigation which show some possibility of furnishing an adequate solution.

It may be necessary to look into the nature of the problem itself before a solution is sought. Analysis is employed to discover its meaning and its applications; and reflection, reading, investigation may be required to make clear what is to be done, and the ways by which the solution is to be attempted. This process of defining the problem and formulating hypotheses for its solution may require a very short time, or it may occupy an extended period. Children's guesses as to what things are, or why things are so and not otherwise, are simply childish hypotheses intended to meet natural situations. The trouble with their studying is that they frequently end their mental efforts merely with the formulation of their problems, rather than accept such formulation as starting points on the way to positive knowledge. The clear understanding of the problem furnishes the criterion for the acceptance or rejection of material, and for its organization. The keener the individual's sense of need, and the more intense his desire to acquire a certain body of knowledge, the clearer his statement of the problem will probably be, and the more definite his demand for what he wants.

*Recognition of the problem the first factor in logical study.*

This recognition of a problem is a factor in proper study, that is, in study in the sense in which we are here considering it; and since it precedes the other steps, it may be called the first factor in study. The problem must originate within the experience of the students, or be appropriated by them in order to arouse thought, and it must be defined clearly in order to furnish a definite guide to thought.

*Summary.*

The points presented thus far are as follows: (1) Teachers should strive for results not only in knowledge of facts but also in knowledge of the process of getting facts. (2) Studying, in its higher meaning, is mental activity directed towards the assimilation of ideas, the reorganization of experience. (3) Proper study involves purposive thinking, since it is thinking that is directed towards some end. (4) Back of the psychological steps involved in studying is the logical basis of the process. This is the tension in experience which constitutes the aim or purpose of thinking, and furnishes the criterion for the acceptance or rejection of ideas in the attempt to readjust experience. (5) The recognition of a problem is the first factor in proper study. (6) This problem must be felt as such by those who are to study, or else the motive and guide for thought are lacking. (7) In order that the thinking may be accurate, the problem must be clearly defined in the mind of the person who is to do the thinking. Its requirements must be plainly perceived, and some hypothesis formed as a tentative explanation. This hypothesis determines the direction which the solution of the problem will take. It should conform to known facts. It should have some reasonable basis.

*Collecting of data a factor in logical study.*

When in the course of experience such a problem as has been described becomes a part of consciousness it controls the nature of the mental process which succeeds it, unless it is inhibited from so doing. One of the most prominent aspects of this process is the gathering of material bearing upon the problem in hand. This collecting of data is a most important factor in logical study; for through its agency we are furnished the means whereby we may prove, amend, or reject the hypotheses formulated for the solution of the problem, and arrive at more definite theories.

The material brought together for these purposes may be drawn from several sources. It may be a part of previous experience that is recalled. It may be information gained from others by inquiry or through reading. It may be material derived through the processes of experimentation and observation. All the resources at our command may be drawn upon in the effort to readjust experience so as to restore harmony. In general, it may be said that too great a reliance upon any one source is unwise. The person who knows nothing but books, and the person who relies entirely upon his own observations are both depriving themselves of material that is valuable; so, also, is the person who is content with what he already knows as the basis for the solution of problems which arise in his life. There is a one-sidedness in such an attitude which defeats the very purpose of thought, i. e., the discovery of truth.

It frequently happens that in this gathering of data, many ideas enter consciousness which are not relevant to the problem and which, therefore, must be rejected; but having clearly defined the problem in the beginning, the sorting process is simplified. We cannot prevent the obtrusion of these irrelevant ideas and it is consequently all the more necessary to learn to discriminate between that which bears upon the problem and that which does not, and to accept or reject accordingly. For example, if a person begins to plan a trip to Europe, the details of other trips are recalled or read, or they may be suggested by friends. Many of these ideas will doubtless be valueless, because they have no bearing upon the problems of the proposed trip, while some may be very helpful. Unless the prospective traveler can sift out the latter and neglect the rest, he will probably do some foolish things, and omit to do some wise ones in making the preparation for his journey.

A consideration of very great importance in regard to data is that they must be gathered from such a number and variety of individual instances as to be sufficiently representative, and hence reliable. For example, data in regard to the physical measurements of Europeans would be very unreliable if obtained from the Anglo-Saxon nations alone, even though many individuals in those nations should be measured. And similarly, measurements to be representative of the English should include all classes of English and not merely a selected group. Likewise, to base all study of the phenomena of the adolescent period upon observations limited to high school students would be manifestly unscientific since high school students are a selected group. Only a small per cent. of pupils entering the first grade ever enter high school. .There is a weeding-out process all along the elementary school course, so that by the time the high school is reached, those who have survived are a chosen few. Studies based upon them alone would not be truly representative of all young people of the same age. It is thus important to remember in considering the reliability of data that they must represent enough individuals and classes to make conclusions based upon them valid.

Summary: The collecting of data is a factor in logical study. Significant facts may be brought into consciousness by recall, by conversation with others, by reading, by experimenting, or by observation. It is unwise to depend upon any one source exclusively. These ideas, however gained, must be judged on the basis of their relevancy to the problem, and accepted or rejected accordingly.

*Organization of ideas a factor in logical study.*

A very important element in logical study is the grouping of related ideas. It is a natural process for ideas to become associated in groups, but in purposive thinking this process must be consciously aided. The ideas accepted because of their bearing upon the problem are examined to discover the nature of their relations to each other. Certain elements of similarity cause certain ideas to form a group, as when concepts are formed. Other ideas are attracted to each other because of the similarity of the relationship which they bear to some other idea. The idea of the navigation laws and the idea of the tax on tea are very dissimilar in nature; but because they both bear a functional relationship to the idea of the Revolutionary War, they are frequently associated in people's minds. Then there is the causal relationship among ideas, when the value of one idea depends upon the value of some preceding idea or series of ideas. For example, the idea of weather-of-a-certain kind becomes associated with the idea of wind-blowing-from-a-certain-direction. Also, in studying parts of speech, the idea of *pronoun* becomes associated with the idea of *noun* because of their logical relationship. These relationships of similarity, of function, of cause and effect, and of place in a logical series, all of which are of importance in the solution of the problem on hand, should be sought out and established. The natural tendency to associate must be supplemented by conscious effort. Furthermore, as a matter of convenience and clearness in dealing with ideas, it is frequently helpful, especially with a long or difficult problem involving much material, to prepare a classification showing the main topics arranged in order, with the subordinate points properly grouped under them. In most of the situations which present us with some problem, no such formal classification is necessary, but undoubtedly much incoherency and lack of logical treatment would be overcome by the more careful arrangement of material employed in attempting to work out some hypothesis.

### Results of the selection and organization of data.

As the result of the selection and organization of data, the hypothesis, which in the beginning was merely a more or less intelligent guess, is much more positive in its nature and has become a theory. Starting with an hypothesis based merely upon the facts immediately connected with the problem, there has been a wide search for data, a careful elimination of the irrelevant, and an organization of that which has been found to bear significantly upon the solution of the problem. During this process, the original hypothesis may have been altered, rejected, or confirmed as a whole or only to a certain extent. Without these two steps, collecting and organizing, the hypothesis would have remained a mere guess. Both hypothesis and theory must be looked upon as tentative conclusions and must be put to the final test of application before being accepted as principles.

### Scientific doubt a factor in logical study.

In the paragraph on the selection of data, it was said that data relevant to the solution of the problem should be accepted. This statement must be modified somewhat. The data must be not only relevant but reliable. Whatever is accepted should be accurate. It frequently happens that material is presented in the working out of a situation which would apparently meet every difficulty, but it lacks the most necessary characteristic—that of accuracy. If the problem to be solved is of any importance to the person who engages in its solution, it is obviously of considerable importance to that person that he accept none but reliable data. He must, then, scrutinize with care that which he accepts, and his attitude in general must be that of doubt. The greater the significance of the problem the more important doubt, scientific doubt, becomes as a factor in study, since freedom from error depends largely upon its existence and exercise. Because much of the information which is obtained from others, whether through their books or their spoken utterances, is based upon incorrect ideas obtained from others, upon faulty experiments, imperfect observations, or false reasoning, and because it is sometimes wilful misrepresentation of facts to accomplish some ulterior motive, those who avail themselves of such sources without investigating the truth of the information imparted are frequently led into error. Ordinary gossip and unprincipled newspapers which are published for political purposes are extreme instances of unreliable sources of information. But even books which are written thoughtfully and with every intention of being accurate contain statements which are biased or untrue. The path of learning is strewn with discarded ideas, theories, hypotheses, which fuller knowledge has shown to be false. The attitude of scientific doubt which opposes blind acceptance of information makes for advance in true knowledge. It should be cultivated so as to counteract the tendency of people in general, especially of young people and of others inexperienced in proving hypotheses and in working out carefully the solution of problems, to accept without question the statements found in books, papers, and magazines, even though they may have learned to exercise some discrimination in regard to what they hear. There are reasons for this attitude of receptivity, but they are not sufficient to warrant the continuance of unquestioning belief since that frequently leads to inaccurate solutions of problems, and quite distorted views of facts.

Our judgment as to the validity of data offered by any author is influenced, or should be influenced by his source of information. In scientific studies, direct observation and experimentation are valued as insuring accuracy. In historical subjects, the use of written evidence, or original sources is a basis for acceptance of statements. In either case, if the author has gained his information through hearsay, there is greater doubt of his reliability as an authority than if he had employed research to obtain his ideas. It is an impossibility to test every statement made by the people to whom we go for information and we therefore must either reject all statements which we cannot verify or else we must place sufficient confidence in the men consulted to accept their presentations. There is a place for the experts in various lines of knowledge; and when men are known to have investigated thoroughly and in scientific spirit in their respective fields of research, there are good reasons why their results should be accepted as authoritative for the time being, at least. There is no loss of self-respect to the student in so doing, and as for verifying data, there is still sufficient opportunity for that since not all people are experts, and not all the problems are yet solved.

The reliability of data can be tested in different ways. Close observation is sometimes all that is necessary; or reflection, comparison, and, in some cases, experimentation may at times be employed. We may recall the results of our own experience and use them as a test for the new; or we may compare one man's statements with those of another in whose methods of working we have confidence, for in weighing evidence it is not so much the men as their methods of working which are to be accepted as authoritative. But, after all is said and done, some doubt is still in place.

*The tentative nature of hypotheses and theories.*

It is very important in studying to recognize the fact that both hypotheses and theories are tentative in their nature although they may differ greatly in degree of probability. An hypothesis is a guess. It may be more or less scientific but it is still a guess. A theory, on the other hand, is an hypothesis which has been carried through the stages of investigation, and perhaps experimentation, and which has been modified or confirmed by the process. It is based upon the study of data, and consequently possesses a greater degree of certainty.

Theories may vary in probability. Where data are lacking, or where there is grave doubt as to their validity, the formation of judgment or theory may be quite suspended for the time being. When evidence is ample in amount and variety and is of such a nature as to warrant it, a very positive, definite theory may be formed. Between these two extremes are theories of varying degrees of certainty. Such theories or judgments are more tentative in nature than those based upon evidence that is complete and positive, though all theories must be looked upon as tentative until verified by experience. When thus verified, they become principles, and serve as bases for decisions in future thinking.

Whenever evidence is doubtful, and yet is accepted because of lack of opportunity for proving it, or for any other reason, the conclusions based upon such data should be regarded as hypothetical rather than theoretical, until doubts of the validity of the data can be removed. Sometimes the material used as the basis for judgment is accurate, but it is not sufficient because it does not meet every requirement of the problem. Conclusions based upon incomplete data should also be held to be lacking in positiveness. While such judgments have value in that they furnish temporary explanations, their incompleteness should be recognized so that the mind of the student may be left open for further progress. Not to recognize them as partial, as tentative, is to become fixed and dogmatic and to close the door to investigation and development. It is equally detrimental to character and learning to accept judgments based upon doubtful or inadequate evidence as final in their nature and to make no further efforts towards positive theories.

Summary: As a precaution by which the way to accuracy of results should be hedged, scientific doubt, or the consideration of the accuracy and reliability of data, must be valued as a factor in study. The data selected in the process of studying because of some bearing upon the problem must be known to be reliable before there can be assurance of validity in the conclusion. This is true of all data, regardless of the source from which or the method by which it is obtained. But even most reliable data are still properly subject to some doubt. Both hypotheses and theories should be regarded as tentative in their nature, and as such, subject to further investigation and proof.

*Verification, or the application of theory, a factor in study.*

Since it was the need of readjustment of some phase of experience which furnished the problem for thought, the verification of the theory formulated must consist in its application to the specific situation which gave rise to the thought-process, or to similar situations. The process of logical study is not completed until the theory has been expressed in some form so as to test its validity; therefore expression, or the execution of theory must be regarded as an element in study.

Application of theory is the only means by which we can be sure that the tension in experience has been removed and the problem solved. Conclusions which cannot stand this test must, of course, be revised or thrown aside, and those which meet the requirements in a satisfactory manner may be accepted. Further-

2

more, the application of theory, if repeated, tends towards facility in its use, and makes it more thoroughly a part of the person who thus employs it.

As was stated in an earlier paragraph, the application of theory may be carried out very carefully, close attention being given both to process and results. If repeated frequently enough without too great a lapse of time between the applications, the process reaches the mechanical stage and becomes a habit which requires little or no conscious effort for its execution. The occurrence of a favorable opportunity for its use usually calls it into activity unless it is inhibited for some reason.

The testing of theories may take the form of using the conclusions as bases for further thinking; it may take the form of some act of construction, the execution of some design embodying the ideas worked out in the thinking process; or it may manifest itself in oral or written expression, in some social activity, or in some other way. A person does certain things because of the conclusions reached; or by an act of will he refrains from doing because his thinking has led him to decide that it is best to do so. Both definite choice and intelligent action are based upon the mental product, and these test the value of that product, and serve as a corrective for careless or inaccurate thinking.

In general, the more genuine the problem has been to the individual who has been studying, the more vital will be the conclusion reached, and the keener the desire to put the results into practice as soon as possible for the sake of verification. In life outside of school, the opportunity for application is sometimes delayed, but if the judgments are strong and clear, they will survive delay and will even force an occasion for use. In school, conditions can frequently be so managed that pupils may apply the results of study immediately; but even there delay is sometimes inevitable. This possibility of postponement is a strong argument in favor of making circumstances as favorable as possible for the formation of clear, vigorous judgments.

Summary: In review of this topic, it may be said that application in some form constitutes the test of theory and is therefore a part of the study process. It is indispensable as a means of verifying, correcting, and fixing conclusions, and of giving facility in their use. Application frequently follows the formulation of theory immediately, though it must sometimes await an opportunity. This possibility of delay increases the necessity of strength and clearness in judgments.

*Memorizing a factor in logical study.*

It is sometimes advisable to remember things in a certain wording or order, and for that reason memorizing forms an important element in study. Whatever conscious memorizing is done to give permanence to thought naturally follows the completion, or at least the partial completion of the thinking process involved in the working out of a situation. The act itself of establishing relationships of meaning among ideas tends to make the ideas thus associated easy of recall, so that by the time a certain problem has been thought through carefully, the ideas involved are already partially memorized in their proper order. Thinking the steps over repeatedly, reviewing the relations already established, completes the memorizing process. Thus memorizing is seen to be a very thoughtful procedure. Its misuse arises in the attempt to substitute it for thought instead of basing it upon thought, and in making it the sole, or at least the main factor in study.

All memorizing takes place through the forming of associations of some kind. These associations may be of a very mechanical and arbitrary nature, as when we learn words in columns, or commit sentences to memory with no idea of their meaning. Mechanical or arbitrary memorizing has its place in school work, since words must be spelled, the principal parts of verbs learned, and other matter of similar nature so fixed that it may be recalled readily when needed. This memorizing involves concentration of attention, the perception of the correct order, and then repetition to fix the ideas in the perceived order.

The memorizing which is a factor in the higher form of studying is based upon associations of meaning among the ideas involved in the study. Similar or contrasting ideas are associated, as are also groups of ideas relating to some one subject; also ideas bearing the relation of cause and effect, and ideas in a logical series. Thus, if a history lesson is to be memorized, it is better to memorize the important facts or topics which have been thought out and associated than it is to learn to recite the words glibly without having had any glimpse into the significance of the ideas expressed. In learning a poem, the process is usually well advanced when the thought of the poem has been mastered. In geography the causal relations, and in mathematics the logical order may form the basis of the memorizing process.

Summary: In general, it may be said that while mechanical memorizing has a certain place in school work, it should be limited to its own legitimate sphere. Thoughtful memorizing is of a higher type and should be employed much more extensively than it now is. It is accomplished by placing emphasis upon associations of meaning rather than upon associations of place. When employed consciously it follows the other steps in proper study.

### The preservation of self in and through studying.

The studying which has been described in the preceding pages affords an opportunity for self-preservation and self-development which mechanical study can never yield. While preservation and development of the individuality are not a separate factor in study, they should be present in study and should be advanced to some extent at least, through its agency.

Human beings vary greatly in native endowments. This variation manifests itself in differences of interests, of capacities for working, and in ways of working. Any method of study which disregards individuals, disregards also these fundamental differences. It subordinates the human being to the subject-matter, and aims for the acquisition of facts rather than for the assimilation of knowledge. In proper study, the individuality of the student has a chance to assert itself. One may respect his own ideas if he has tested them and has found that they satisfy the requirements. He need not yield ready acceptance to all that he hears or reads or thinks, but may reject what is false or irrelevant. He need not lose his identity or his respect for himself even though he does accept the ideas of others, provided the acceptance follows judgment of value. He need be no one's tool or blind follower, but may learn to esteem ideas because of their worth rather than because of their source. He needs to learn the distinction between beliefs and convictions, but having the latter, he may have courage in the face of any amount of opposition. To be alone in one's views is not necessarily to be in error, while to fall in with popular views is to place one's self very frequently in the wrong. Even though a number of people should start to solve the same problem and should employ in general the factors of study here presented, their procedure would vary from stage to stage because of differences which would manifest themselves at every step.

A very important element in the development and preservation of self is the exercise of initiative; the higher form of study affords excellent opportunities for the manifestation of this activity. The recognition of a problem, the selection and discrimination of data, the organization of ideas, the deferring of judgment, the formulation of theory or hypothesis, the consideration of the truth or falsity of statements, and the final testing of theory involve its use. The highest ideals formulated by educational theory include the right training of whatever initiative man has been endowed with; hence so excellent an opportunity for its proper use as is furnished by logical study should not be neglected.

Summary: In studying, it is an important consideration to preserve and develop one's personality, to exercise initiative, and not to subordinate one's own ideas to those of others without due consideration; otherwise one becomes a mental nonentity, a " passive recipient," and the whole process of study loses its value as a means of training and as a means of arriving at truth.

General summary: The points made thus far are, in brief, as follows: (1) The first factor in logical study is the recognition of a problem. The problem must be clearly understood and its implications recognized. To arrive at a clear understanding it may be necessary to reflect, consult others, read, or experiment and observe. Some hypothesis or hypotheses may be formulated as possible solutions of the problem. (II) A second factor in study is the gathering of data bearing upon the problem. This material may be gathered from many sources, but only that which bears a relation to the problem should be accepted. (III) The organization of material into groups of related ideas is a third factor of study. It tends to take place naturally, but should be carried on consciously with close attention given to the relationships established. As the result of (II) and (III) we are able to formulate a theory which is intended to satisfy the problem. (IV) A fourth factor in study is the exercise of scientific doubt, or judging as to the soundness of statements. Whenever significant facts bearing upon the problem are presented to consciousness, their validity should be determined in order that the theory based upon such evidence may have value. All hypotheses and theories must be considered as tentative judgments until verified by experience. The value of such judgments is that application or further investigation is encouraged, and the tendency to form positive judgments upon a slight or faulty basis is discouraged. (V) In order to verify the conclusions reached in the process of logical thinking, a fifth factor in study is needed. This is application, or the execution of theory. Through the use of this factor of study, theories are rejected, corrected, or accepted according as they meet the conditions of the original problem which gave rise to the thought-situation, or of similar problems. Through use, also, the theory is fixed as an element of knowledge and the expression becomes habitual. (VI) To fix knowledge in a certain form memorizing is necessary, and this process, accordingly, makes a sixth factor in study. Thoughtful memorizing is accomplished in part during the course of the thinking process. It is completed by consciously attending to the relationships to be fixed in mind and by reviewing them in their logical order. (VII) Throughout the process of logical study, there is opportunity for the preservation and development of the individuality of the student. This is as it should be since training in process is fully as much needed in life as the accumulation of facts, though the facts are not to be despised. Logical study calls for individual effort and individual judgment and affords opportunity for the exercise of initiative. Training in its use is training in the use of native power and ability to the best advantage. Like results need not be expected, therefore, in all cases, since minds differ in native endowment, in the nature of the store of knowledge already acquired, in the ways of judging data and in the modes of making application.

NOTE.—For a fuller discussion of the ideas in regard to the thought-situation presented in this chapter see *Studies in Logical Theory,* by Professor John Dewey.

# CHAPTER II

## THE NATURE OF LOGICAL STUDY—CONTINUED

*The deductive form of logical study.*

The logical study thus far described has begun with some problem and has advanced toward the formulation of the theory which provides the solution for it. The process is inductive in nature, and being so, is applicable in the large number of occasions in life in which the formulation of some theory is necessary to explain facts. However, problems are not always of this nature; they sometimes require the employment of theories or principles which have already been formulated. The facts are before us and call, not for the formulation of a new theory, but for the use of one which is known. Examples of this form of thinking are seen in recognition, interpretation, and in any use of formulated knowledge. Effort in such cases is directed towards identifying the fact present in consciousness with some group of facts for which a satisfactory theory already exists. Through this identification, we read into the fact the significance or meaning of the principle which is applied to it. The mathematician who sees that the facts given in his problem involve a certain principle or rule; the scientist who identifies some plant or animal as belonging to some group he already knows; and the pupil who recognizes some part of speech as a noun, and who consequently attributes to it the properties of nouns,—all these are employing principles, theories, or classifications already formulated. The process is one of application rather than of discovery of theory. It is deductive in its nature. It is very frequently employed in giving explanations of facts or situations, though the full form of deductive reasoning is often cut short by assuming part of the steps. For example, in determining the climate of a given place, certain facts about location, physiography, winds, and altitude are cited, the assumption being that all places having these features have a certain kind of climate; and that the given place, having these conditions, must therefore have the same kind of climate as all the other places similarly conditioned.

*Necessity of understanding the problem.*

In this deductive process of studying there is the same need of recognition and analysis of the problem as in the inductive study. Without a clear understanding of the situation, there is no adequate criterion for the selection of the theory or principle which is to furnish the solution, since its relevancy is not apparent until the problem has been made plain.

*Judging the adequacy of a principle or theory.*

In the purely deductive process of studying, the factor—judging the soundness of statements—may not play so important a part as in the inductive study. It depends upon the extent to which data are employed. In deductive study it is the theory which must undergo criticism, and we must judge of its applicability, its adequacy, to the solution of the problem. A theory or principle may be relevant but not adequate, and it becomes necessary to discriminate between that which is sufficient to furnish the desired solution, and that which is not.

Sometimes, however, a final judgment as to the theory or principle must be deferred, either because the problem itself has not been completely analyzed, or because no adequate theory has been formulated, or because we are not able to find the right theory. We must then either accept a judgment or classification tentatively, or we must try to remove the difficulty which has prevented the definite acceptance of a solution as adequate and final. This may be done by further study of the conditions of the problem itself, by an inductive study of the theory, or by a further search for a theory which has already been formulated.

*Application of theory.*

The test by which the adequacy of a theory is determined is its application to the situation which caused the search for a theory. As long as theories are never applied to problems, it matters little which ones are selected; but little progress is made by this plan. The more genuine and vital the problem, the greater the need of the application of whatever theory is selected after careful examination. Thus the chemist or physician who attempts to produce a serum for tetanus or rabies, proceeds upon certain principles believed to have been established through the discovery of other serums. Having obtained the serums according to principle, he usually applies them first to some animals to test their efficacy. The bridgebuilder or the boatbuilder who seeks to meet a new or peculiar situation, not only searches for his theory or principle, but frequently tests it in the manufacture of a model before using it in the actual situation. The final test, however, is its use in the connection for which it was intended.

The collection and organization of data, factors of study employed when the process was inductive, are present in deductive study also. They appear in the analysis and delimitation of the problem itself, and in the selection and study of other examples manifesting the same peculiarities as the one which gave rise to the problem. The search for data and their careful study leads to the discovery of the principle whose application they illustrate. The expression " discovery of principle " as here employed, does not mean formulation of theory, but rather the finding of a theory which has already been formulated and which furnishes the explanation of the problem.

Logical memorizing is also present in deductive study, though it may not always be as prominent or as necessary as in the inductive process. The results of previous memorizing are employed and thus the thoroughness of the process is tested. In the new work, the relation of the data giving rise to the problem to the theory which solves the problem, may call for memorizing to fix the relation for future use. In such cases it should not be neglected.

*Self-expression and self-development through deductive study.*

Whenever there is a genuine problem present which is felt as such by the student, and whenever the factors of logical study are employed freely by him, there is opportunity for the expression and development of self. It requires initiative in deductive study as well as in inductive, to discover the problem, see its implications and conditions, and find and test the solution. Where, however, the process is purely formal, and is carried on under the direction and dictation of another, the higher thinking powers of the student remain inactive, and consequently undeveloped. Such formal use of theory is seen in the application of rules, principles, or definitions in mathematics, grammar, or physics when the pupils have little idea of the meaning of the problems and possibly none at all of the rules, definitions and principles.

In conclusion, we may say that the factors present in inductive study are present in deductive study also, though they may be modified to suit the changed purpose of the study, which is to apply principles rather than to formulate theory.

# CHAPTER III

## RELATION OF LOGICAL STUDY TO THE STUDY OF THE TEXTBOOK

In the preceding chapters, the steps or factors in logical study, both inductive and deductive, have been described and illustrated. The discussion has been general in its nature, as it was thought best to see the broad significance of study before confining the attention to the form it takes under certain limitations.

Schoolroom conditions and traditional procedure are the limitations which hedge in the pupils in the years devoted to so-called study. In the ordinary schoolroom we find a group of pupils of nearly the same age, pursuing the same subjects from the same books, and with freedom of physical activity at least greatly restricted. The question is pertinent here as to whether the factors present in purely logical study are possible in the study of the textbook. Some reflection upon the nature of textbook work shows that to a large extent these factors may be employed, though in a modified form.

*Consciousness of the author's problem or purpose the first factor in textbook study.*

First of all in systematic textbook study, as in other study, there is the necessity of some problem. In ordinary experience aside from books, the problem is found in some life situation, but in the book the author provides it and the student must find and appropriate it. An author may have written a chapter of psychology to'show the nature, kinds, and uses of interest; of geography to show how the mountains of Europe affect the climate and drainage of that continent; or of history to show how New England came to be settled by the Puritans. The problem was present in the author's mind and was worked out by him in some section of his book. The student must re-discover it, and appropriate it for his own in order that he may benefit by his study. His question to himself must be, "What was the author's purpose in writing this?" or "What is the main thought of this section?" or "What underlying idea runs all through this chapter, connecting the various parts?" Through some such

self-questioning and self-directing of thought, the author's purpose or problem is revealed, whether in geography, history,
grammar, arithmetic or some other subject.

*Gathering data a factor in textbook study.*

When the author's aim has been grasped, the gathering of
data is necessary in textbook study, just as it is in any situation
where there is a problem to solve. In the use of the book, however, the author supplies much of the material that is to be
used, and the student must look upon it as data presented with
the idea of solving the author's problem. The student is not
limited to the author's text, however, but may draw upon his
own experience and upon his imagination. He may read books,
papers, magazines, and may talk with people who are informed
in regard to the subject he is studying. He may perform experiments and make observations. In any or all of these ways
he may supplement the author's text and add largely to the
material bearing upon his problem. The criterion for acceptance
is here as in other study the relevancy to the problem of the
facts presented to consciousness. That which is irrelevant should
be rejected, and only the relevant accepted. If, for example,
the problem is, " How the mineral products of the western states
have influenced the development of those states," then students
engaged upon such a problem may neglect all the statements
made by the author which do not bear upon this problem, but
they must sift out and accept that which contributes to its solution.

*Organization of ideas a factor in textbook study.*

The step of organizing ideas differs in textbook study from
the organizing that is done when the student must seek and
accept data which have not already been organized. Textbooks
present a certain form of organization and the student must discover it in order to see fully the author's treatment of his
problem. This includes finding the main points in the chapter or
paragraph involved in the problem, and in grouping the related
minor points about these main points. This organization of the
text may be extended or otherwise changed by the use of supplementary material which the student has gathered and accepted
as bearing upon the author's problem. An example of organi-

zation of textbook material is the following: Examination of a section in a textbook in United States history shows the author's problem to be the explanation of how slavery was introduced into the United States. Further study shows a number of details which group themselves into a few points:

I. How slavery was introduced into the United States.
   1. Reasons for its introduction.
   2. The introduction of negroes as slaves.
      A. Time.
      B. Place.
      C. Agency.
   3. The introduction of indentured servants.
      A. Reason for practice.
      B. Character of these servants.
      C. The end of white slavery in America.

Such organization not only shows the author's mode of treatment of his subject but it also enables the student to handle his material more conveniently. It brings out the main points clearly, and about these can be grouped the needed details. The irrelevant and the unimportant are weeded out. As a result of organization the author's theory as to the solution of his problem should have been grasped by the person who is studying.

*The necessity of deferred judgment in the study of books.*

The same caution which is necessary in logical study in general in regard to accepting hypotheses and theories as provisional rather than final conclusions, is necessary also in the study of books. The same conservatism, also, in forming such theories is necessary. Forming hasty judgments and jumping at conclusions are of frequent enough occurrence in such subjects as literature, history, and other subjects to show the need of greater discretion in this direction. It frequently happens that judgments of persons or actions, or of other matters, are formed before the situation has been sufficiently worked out by the author to make the formulation of theory possible. To anticipate the course of history so as to introduce the results of a movement at the place where its beginning is described is not always feasible or advisable, and so final judgment of its significance should be deferred until adequate knowledge has been acquired. Any other judgment must be regarded as mere hypothesis. Final judgment of character in literature or history must await the development of events sufficiently to warrant it. The results of some treaties and laws are so far-reaching that immediate judgments as to their value would probably be erroneous. Geography, also, frequently calls for the use of caution in drawing conclusions. To judge of climate on the grounds of latitude alone, and to think that because the people of the Western States are far removed from the Atlantic seaboard they are therefore uncultured and live in primitive style, are manifestly rash acts of judgment, yet such judgments are not uncommon. Further data would doubtless cause the correction of one hypothesis and the abandonment of the other.

If children are permitted to do so, they frequently ask their teachers for reasons and explanations, showing that they are aware of lack of fulness in their books and that they desire further data. Here again it happens that the forming of a positive theory must await the right opportunity for the acquisition of knowledge. In the end, the ideas gathered may not be sufficient to warrant the formulation of theory, and if any judgment is formed it must be an hypothesis. But the elements of tentativeness in both hypotheses and theories must not be lost sight of, nor the need of final verification.

*Consideration of the soundness of statements a factor in the study of a book.*

The attitude of scientific doubt which manifests itself in the consideration of the soundness of statements and the validity of data of any kind is quite as essential a factor in textbook study as in any other. If it was necessary to scrutinize statements with a critical eye when the textbook was but one of several sources from which facts were sought, it is the more necessary to exercise care when the book becomes the main source of data bearing upon the problem. Histories, grammars, geographies, and other texts have been known to contain inaccurate material, and even the truth is at times so startling as to cause a challenge in the mind of the readers. For example, a certain text in grammar gives the following definition of a phrase: " A phrase is any combination of words that does not include both subject and predicate."[1] Then any group of words selected at random might form a phrase, if only no subject and predicate are included. This second definition makes the weakness of the first one more clear: "A phrase is a group of related words without subject and predicate, and having the use of a single word."[2] The following statement in regard to the Russian peasants is taken from a geography textbook published before the recent Russo-Japanese war and still in use: "It was not until 1863 that serfdom was abolished. Hence it is no wonder that the masses are without education; but great progress is now being made."[3] A certain textbook in United States history, in treating of the opening events of the Civil War, says: "But the attack on Fort Sumter changed the whole situation. Doubt was at an end on both sides. Virginia, North Carolina, Tennessee, and Arkansas forced now to take one side or the other, soon joined the Confederacy."[4] The question might well be asked, "What was the situation in the border states where both sides were represented? Was all doubt ended there by the attack on Fort Sumter?" Furthermore, the statements that "We are to remember that, though the war was caused by slavery, it was not at first about slavery, but about secession,"[5] and "The Southerners were naturally more military than the Northern people,"[6] are somewhat startling to the pupils who have been taught up to this time that slavery was the cause of the war and have heard little or nothing of secession, and who have believed the Northern men to be in every way equal if not superior to the men of the South. Such statements should challenge pupils to question and investigate their worth. The author's accounts or explanations may be compared with one's own experience. His use of sources and his method of treating problems need to be considered to determine whether he works cautiously. or is hasty in his judgments. It is often worth while to ask the question, "What is the writer's authority for the statements he makes?" "Does he base his conclusions upon observation, upon written evidence, or is he relying upon hearsay?" These questions are frequently in order

[1]Welsh, *Lessons in English*, p. 34.
[2]Webster, *Elements of English Grammar*, p. 39.
[3]The Werner Grammar School Geography, Part I, p. 244.
[4]Eggleston, *Household History of the United States*, p. 310.
[5]Ibid, p. 311.
[6]Ibid, p. 312.

in the study of history, geography, and the natural sciences. Other books and sources of information may be consulted as a means of verification or correction. Caution is especially necessary if magazine articles and newspapers are used as texts in studying certain subjects or phases of subjects.

It is not intended that pupils shall question everything they read or hear. Usually they will not need to have doubts as to the reliability of the statements made. But the attitude of ready acceptance of everything needs to be replaced by the attitude of mind which questions that which seems out of harmony with previous experience, which is startling in its nature, which seems to lack sufficient evidence, or which seems too general in its scope. Such instances, and possibly others, furnish occasion for thought and investigation as to the validity of the material offered. In this respect, textbook study does not differ from any other study in which data are presented to throw light upon some situation. Judgment as to the soundness of statements is usually necessary though due credence should be given to the results of the labors of experts in the several fields of knowledge.

### Verification or the application of theory a factor in the study of the textbook.

The use of verification as a factor in studying books is frequently modified by the fact that the author makes his own application of the theory he has advanced. But because the books are textbooks they are limited in the amount of space that can be devoted to any part of a subject, and consequently that which is given to verification of theory is usually small, and the amount and variety of material presented for giving facility in the application is often inadequate. There is much that can and should be done to apply the theories presented in the books and rediscovered by the pupils to life-situations in which the latter participate. Real occasions for the use of arithmetical ideas and correct grammatical constructions are possible. All of the forms of expression described under this topic in the consideration of logical study are applicable in textbook study, whether it be oral or written expression, constructive work, social activity, some application to the affairs of ordinary life, or even the use of the theory as the basis for further thought. One need only recognize the value of application as a factor in higher study and look for opportunities for employing it and frequently some appropriate form will be found. As was said in a previous chapter, the time for using the theory may be delayed until a favorable opportunity arrives, but often the verification may be made as soon as the theory is clearly understood. Strength and clearness of the ideas are very necessary in order that these may function when there is an opportunity for them to do so.

### Memorizing as a factor in study.

With ideas selected and associated through the use of the factors of study already discussed, memorizing of the logical type has already been included to some extent. Its further use in the study of material selected from textbooks does not differ from the memorizing described under logical study. Its use is both possible and advisable in such a connection.

### Deductive study of books.

So much of the study of books in school is deductive in its character that but little time need be devoted to its explanation here. Parsing and sentential analysis in grammar, the solution of problems in mathematics, the explanations of geographical phenomena, and the interpretation of history all involve the calling up of principles, rules, theories or other general forms of knowledge and the application of them to concrete instances. The criticism has been made that this form of logical study has been over-emphasized in school and that pupils have been expected to apply general ideas which they do not clearly understand. Since both inductive and deductive study are possible in school work, it may be said in general that when pupils are found to lack the general knowledge needed for the solution of problems, the inductive form of study should be employed; but that when the pupils possess the principles needed for explanation or interpretation the deductive form of study should be used. The two methods might thus be used in the same study period in connection with the same lesson, or they may not thus occur. It depends upon the nature of the lesson and the mental equipment of the pupils how frequently and closely they are associated.

3

*Relation of proper textbook study to initiative and self-development.*

Although the use of books does not afford the same opportunity for the use of one's own powers, nor provide the same motives and interests as the study which arises from life-situations where the problems are felt to be of moment, yet they do furnish a means for self-development and self-expression if they are rightly used. It is for the purpose of furthering this right use that the explanations of this chapter have been given. If one would be helped by the use of books, he must master them and not be mastered by them; i. e. he must weigh, judge, test before he accepts their statements, or else he loses his own individuality. It requires the exercise of initiative to discover the problems in books, just as it does to discover them in logical study aside from books. It requires it, also, to select, accept, reject, and organize data, and grasp the author's theory. One of the highest expressions of the self will be found in the testing of statements and in the recognition of judgments as tentative because of faulty or inadequate data. And so, also, in the form of application which the student employs there is opportunity for the development of his own personality, provided he be free to exercise choice as to its form.

If textbook study be limited to rote learning or to deductive study, the opportunities for the exercise of initiative and self-expression are greatly limited. Since the school's recognized function is to further the wise development of these powers of the pupils, it should not neglect so valuable an agency as the higher form of study offers. If study could be directed in genuine life-situations where problems of real importance to pupils abound, the opportunities for self-expression and development would be most favorable. But textbook study is not devoid of possibilities in this direction and these possibilities should be recognized and utilized.

Before leaving this discussion of the use of systematic study in connection with school work, the question should be considered as to whether all of the factors of higher study are necessary in all study. The answer must be a decided negative. First of all, as was pointed out in the first chapter, a great deal of school work does not deal with the assimilation of knowledge but with the mastery of technique: for example, spelling, mechanical

work in arithmetic, and the formal side of reading. There the mechanical side prevails and the readjustment of ideas based upon their thought-relations is not involved. In the second place, much of the subject-matter which does involve the relationship of ideas based upon meaning is of such a nature as to present little of value in the way of problems. It is intended to entertain, or to cultivate taste and sentiment rather than to furnish food for thought. Some school histories, books about nature, and a good deal of the reading matter and literature put before pupils belong to this class. They present few logical problems of value and call for little purposive thinking. Whether they should do so to a greater extent than is now the case, is a question worthy of consideration, as is also the question as to whether the logical possibilities, slight though they are, should not be more fully realized. Even in subjects or subject-matter which call for systematic study there are great differences in the nature and importance of problems presented from time to time. Not all problems are worth the time and effort involved in the use of all the factors of study; and some may not require the use of all in order to reach a solution which is entirely satisfactory. Frequently minor problems present themselves during the study of larger ones. It is sometimes necessary to ignore them entirely or to postpone their consideration to some other time. If their solution is indispensable to the main problem in hand, then time and attention must be given to them as to other problems.

It may be said, further, that some problems may involve several or all of the factors of systematic study and yet be solved quickly, while other problems may require a long time for solution, being taken up for consideration from time to time as circumstances determine. For some reason the gathering of data may be deferred, and meanwhile the problem rests unsolved; or delay may be due to some other cause. In general it may be said that the length of time spent in studying problems varies. Several may be disposed of in one study period, or one may extend through a long period, being considered from time to time as the work develops.

# CHAPTER IV

## The Ability of Children in the Elementary School to Study

Having seen the nature of logical study and having followed the application of its various steps to the mastery of a lesson in a book, it is of great importance to know whether children are capable of studying in the manner described. Can children see the author's problem, or find the underlying thought running through a lesson? Can they collect material bearing upon this problem? Can they find the important points in a chapter, or paragraph, or other section, offering a problem? Can they question statements, and see discrepancies in the material offered? Can they, in general, employ the various factors of logical study? If mechanical study is the only kind of which children in the elementary schools are capable, then the whole discussion of study down to this point is irrelevant as far as they are concerned.

*Factors influencing the preparation of the experiments to determine the ability of pupils to study.*

The attempt to find an adequate answer to the questions in the preceding paragraph involved the consideration of many serious difficulties. The grades, the number of children, the location of the schools, the subjects to be used in testing, the nature of the exercises, and the manner of conducting them—all these and various other points had to be determined before the tests could be given. The situation was made even more complicated by the desire to train part of the classes in systematic study after the first tests had been given, and then to give all pupils, both trained and untrained, a second series similar to the first, with the purpose of finding out what differences were to be observed in the results obtained from the two classes of pupils.

The desire to give part of the pupils some training in systematic study necessarily determined the location where some of the tests should be given, since the training must be conducted under the direction of those who were familiar with the theory of study which was the subject of experimentation. This theory had been presented in the year 1905-06 by Professor F. M. McMurry before a class in Teachers College, Columbia University. This class was composed entirely of experienced teachers, and to these teachers the appeal for assistance was made during the year 1906-07. Only part of those appealed to were able to promise help, but through these teachers certain classes in Baltimore, Md., Passaic, N. J., Westport, Conn., and in the Training Department of the State Normal School in Macomb, Ill., were secured. Two teachers in the Speyer School, the School of Practice of Teachers College, agreed to attempt the training of their classes, also. In addition to the classes already mentioned, others were obtained for testing without training in the public schools of New York City, of Passaic, N. J., and of Indianapolis, Ind.

The subject of geography was chosen for the tests, both because it furnishes abundant opportunities for proper study, and also because it is a subject which is quite sure to be taught in all of the higher grades of the elementary schools. History is not taught so generally as geography, and for this reason was not selected for the experiments. The ideal procedure would have been to train the pupils in the method of study in connection with all of their school subjects, and to test them in all of these, but while the teacher might have trained them in all branches offering opportunities for logical study, the testing would have been too arduous and too time-consuming, especially since more than a thousand pupils were tested.

The tests were given to pupils of the sixth and seventh grades only. Pupils in these grades are supposed to be able to express themselves sufficiently well in writing to be able to work upon the material given. The eighth grade was not chosen because of the possibility of wishing to give similar tests during the following year, in which case, the eighth grade pupils would not have been available because they would have left the elementary school.

In order to make the results as general as possible, the tests were given to as many classes as could be obtained for the purpose. More than twelve hundred pupils wrote upon the first series, which was given early in the year 1907. When the second test was given three months later, several classes dropped out, and the number was reduced to about eleven hundred. In each pair of tests, only those results were considered which were obtained from pupils present in both of them.

## *The nature of the tests employed.*

Five different kinds of tests were given so that both the subjective and objective sides of the studying might be observed. It seemed as if the studying process employed might be more clearly seen if the pupils not only described their way of studying but also performed some work which tested their ability to employ the various factors of study. The tabulation of the results of two of the tests has not yet been completed.

The subject-matter used in the tests was selected from geography textbooks intended for use in the elementary schools. The *Redway and Hinman,* the *Tarr and McMurry,* the *Frye,* the *Dodge,* and the *Werner* texts were all drawn upon for material.

Ten tests were given to each of the two grades selected, five being given in the first series, and five in the second. The requirements for the corresponding tests in the two series were alike in nature. In preparing each one of these tests, material was selected for five tests, as nearly equal in interest and difficulty as possible. Each of these fifty tests was prepared as if to be presented to a class, and then from each of the ten groups of five, two tests were drawn at random, the first one drawn being laid aside for the first test in that group, and the second one drawn being used for the second series. Each test with directions as to how it was to be used was then printed, so that each pupil who wrote the tests had his own printed slip containing the subject-matter and directions.

The first test in each series was probably the most difficult. It consisted of a short selection from one of the geography textbooks and was accompanied by the following requirement: " Here is a lesson from a book such as you use in class. Do whatever you think you ought to do in studying this lesson thoroughly, and then tell (write down) the different things you have done in studying it. Do not write anything else." If the other tests had been given first, they would probably have influenced the pupils in the preparation of this one; so this one was given first. It was hoped that the results would show whether any pupils were employing the factors of logical study, and to what extent they were employing them.

In connection with this test, which was called test A,[1] these directions were sent to the teachers: "When test A is given, the class should be observed as it works, and notes should be taken as to what the different pupils do. If a pupil gets one or more books for reference, consults the dictionary, sits and thinks, etc., it should be noted, so that the teacher's notes can be compared with the child's account of what he has done. These notes should be forwarded with the test papers when they are completed. Test A is the only one in which the pupils may be permitted to consult books, and they are to do that in test A only if they think of it themselves."

The second test in each series, test B,[2] consisted of a few paragraphs of subject matter from a textbook. The pupils were instructed to write a list of the important questions whose answers were found in the lesson. This exercise was intended to test the pupils' ability to discriminate between the important and the relatively unimportant ideas in the lesson.

In the third test, test C,[3] the pupils were given a question with this direction: "Do not answer this question, but write down everything you think you ought to do in finding the answer to it." For the first series in the sixth grade the question was, "Why is Pittsburg such an important commercial and manufacturing city?" For the second series, it was the following: "Tobacco used to be grown almost entirely in the Southern States, but now it is grown extensively in the Northern States as well. Why has this change come about?" In the first series for the seventh grade the question was: "Why do terrible famines occur in India every few years?" In the second series, the pupils were asked, "If you were a voter and a governor was to be elected in your State, how would you decide which of the candidates to vote for?"

Test C, like test A, instead of making some definite requirement of the pupils, emphasized the subjective side of the problem. In test A the pupils were to tell what they had done; in test C they were to tell what they would do. The object was the same, that is, to discover to what extent the pupils were employing the factors of logical study.

In the fourth test, test D,[4] the pupils were given the slip con-

---

[1]See Appendix.
[2]See Appendix.
[3]See Appendix.
[4]See Appendix.

taining subject-matter from a text-book.  The accompanying
direction was: " Study this lesson until you think you know it,
and then return it to your teacher."  When the first slip was returned, a second one was given to the pupils.  This second slip
contained questions about the text which had just been studied.
These questions were of such a nature that they did not permit
of *verbatim* answers, but required rather that the important facts
stated in the lesson be used in framing the answers.  This exercise was intended to test the mastery of the main points in a
lesson, rather than the memorizing of the words.

The last test in each series, test E,[1] called directly for systematic study of a lesson.  It consisted of a slip containing subject
matter from a textbook, and an accompanying slip containing the
directions and requirements, both slips being given to the pupils
at the same time.  The pupils were to find the answers to the
following questions, numbering them as the questions are numbered:

1. What is the subject of this lesson?
2. Write a list of the principal topics in it.
3. What do you think is the most important thing in this lesson?
4. What are your reasons for thinking this so important?
5. What other facts do you know about any of these topics?
6. What questions would you ask in regard to anything in this
lesson that is not clear to you or that you would like to know
more about?

This test was placed at the end of the series so that it might
not serve as a clue in the writing of any of the other exercises.

Directions in regard to the manner of conducting the tests[2]
were sent to each principal in whose building the tests were to
be given.  In general, these directions were intended to exclude
all talking by the teacher; to provide that the pupils work without assistance of any kind from any person; that each child
should have all the time he needed for the completion of the
test; and that the tests should be given during the forenoons of
successive days.  Instructions were given as to how the head-

[1]See Appendix.
[2]See Appendix.

ing of all papers was to be written, and in regard to other details of the preparation of the papers.

Each child's time record was to be indicated on the heading, and the directions said: " Each child should have as much time as he needs for each test, * * * Begin to count time after the heading is written. Be sure each child indicates it." These directions proved not to be sufficiently explicit, so that the time records do not all have the same meaning. They therefore possess little value as a basis for comparison.

## Test A.

Table I[1] shows the results obtained by an examination of the papers written for test A. The sixth and seventh grades are separated in this report, as are also the classes in each grade which were trained in systematic studying during the three months which elapsed between the first and second series of tests.

In preparing this test, most of the pupils did one of four things. They followed the directions exactly, or they wrote down the results of their study, or they told what they would do in studying a lesson, or they wrote the facts of the lesson either in the form of a *verbatim* reproduction or more briefly. Sometimes two or more of these modes of treatment were found combined on the same paper. The reports of what the pupils said they would do were kept quite distinct from the reports which showed what had been done; but they were considered as having value in that they revealed the ideas of the pupils in regard to studying. Probably some of the pupils actually did the things which they said they would do, and used the wrong tense in reporting it. It may have been the case, also, that some of the pupils either did not have their textbooks and books of reference, or they may not have felt free to use them without permission. One teacher reported that the pupils used books " stealthily," and in that class only a few reported that they had used books, and the number who said that they would use them was not much larger. Another teacher reported thus: " Before the pupils were permitted to look at the printed test, they were told that ordinarily they must wait for permission of teachers to take books out, or to go to the closet for material. For this

---

[1]See Appendix.

work they had permission to do anything they found necessary in order to do the work." This teacher did not follow the direction about refraining from all explanations or talk of any kind, but her suggestion and the freedom permitted to the class resulted in more than forty per cent. of the class using books of some kind, while others reported that they would use them, bringing the total per cent. up to nearly fifty.

*Factors of logical study shown in Test A.*

The various items in Tables I, II, and III[1] were arranged after an examination of several sets of papers, and not according to some preconceived scheme. Those in Table I which show most clearly the use of the factors of logical study are the ones in regard to finding the subject, finding the most important points, verifying statements, supplementing the lesson, and preparing questions.

*The extent to which the pupils tested found the subject.*

In the first series, a total of 14 reported that they had found the subject, or the work on their papers showed that they had found it. In the second test, 25 reported similarly. If we add to these totals the number who reported that they would find the subject, they become 16 and 26 respectively, or 1.9% and 4.3% of the whole number of pupils writing both tests. How many pupils unintentionally concealed what they did by saying that they " thought," or " tried to understand," or that they " studied the lesson," cannot be estimated; but the number of those who possessed the ability to find the subject is shown by an examination of Table III.

*The ability of the pupils to find the subject.*

In test E, the results of which are included in Table III, the requirement was made to find the subject of the lesson, and the total results are very different from those given in Table I. In test E of the first series, 301 pupils or 36.4%, found a subject which was considered adequate; and in the second series, 114 answers or 13.8% of the whole, were similarly marked. The sixth grade in writing test E of the first series gave in most cases a subject which included but part of the lesson, many of them

---

[1]See Appendix.

giving *Rivers* as the subject. In the second series, they reversed themselves, and gave a subject which was too general, most of them saying that *Georgia* was the subject. On the whole, but few of the subjects were irrelevant, and there were almost no failures to give a subject of some kind.

The results of the two tests indicate that while these pupils do not find the subject of the lesson to any great extent when studying without definite directions, they are capable to a considerable extent of finding it when they are required to do so.

*The tendency and ability of pupils to organize subject-matter.*

In regard to finding the most important points or facts in the lesson, Table I shows that in test A the number of pupils who either actually gave these facts, or said they found them, is 88, or 10.4%, for the first series, and 171, or 20.2% for the second. Adding those who said they would find them, the numbers become 109, or 12.9% for the first series; and 226, or 26.8% for the second. In test E, where the pupils were directed to write a list of the principal topics, the response was better, even though in this test, the replies were classified as adequate or inadequate. Table III shows that in the first series 265, or 32%, prepared adequate lists of topics; while in the second series 214, or 28.8%, did so. The number of those who prepared no lists is very small, being less than 2% in either test.

In judging of the adequacy of a list of principal topics, two questions were kept in mind: Do the topics cover the entire lesson? Do they include the main points only, or are they too detailed? Some pupils gave topics which were very good as far as they went, but they left out some important section of the lesson. For example, in test E of the second series, a number of children omitted to include a topic which would cover the last paragraph, the paragraph which tells about the homes of the different races, or, how the houses of the races are separated from each other. On the other hand, some pupils prepared a topic for nearly every sentence in the lesson. Such lists as these could not be reckoned as adequate because they were either too meagre or because they were too detailed in nature. However, even such lists show some degree of ability, and taken into consideration with those who prepared adequate lists, they show that these children are able, in varying degrees of efficiency, to analyze a lesson and find the essential facts in it.

### *The extent to which pupils questioned or verified the author's statements.*

Table I shows that few children thought of questioning the author's statements while writing test A. In the first series 7, and in the second series 10, reported that they either had verified or would verify the text. One boy reported, " The next thing I did was to find out if everything was true what the paper said." Others referred to the maps or texts to see if the statements about the proximity of Africa to Europe and Asia were true. One child said, " I found out that Europe and Asia were really almost near each other. I found this out in my Natural Advanced Geography."

In test E, the opportunity for doubt was given in the sixth question: " What questions would you ask in regard to anything in this lesson that is not clear to you or that you would like to know more about?" A good many questions were asked which are answered in the text placed before the pupils. These might indicate doubt as to the reliability of the statements read, but probably few of them do so. For example, in the sixth grade, in test E of the second series, the following questions were written: " Was Atlanta the capital of Georgia?" " What is Savannah noted for?" " Is Savannah situated on the coast of Georgia?" " What is eighteen miles from the ocean?" " What are the chief exports?" These are probably merely memory questions asked rather as a matter of form than because the pupils wished confirmation of the statements of the exercise. A very few pupils showed genuine difficulty in accepting the text. One child wrote: " The question is not clear to me because you say that Savannah was taken by the British during the Revolutionary War. And when I studied the geography I found that Savana was in Georgia and belonged to the U. S. So please let me no how it happened that U. S. got it back." One pupil in the seventh grade, when writing about the races of people, expressed herself as follows: " It says that America is the home of the Indians, and down below it says that the land of the Indians is bounded on all sides by the sea. I disagree with this answer."

On the whole, the pupils accepted the subject-matter placed before them without questioning its accuracy. The tests do not reveal any power the children in these classes may possess of seeing discrepancies between what they read and what they know. Whether they really possess this power and would exercise it if permitted or required to do so is a point left undecided by these two exercises.

*The ability to supplement the text of the lesson.*

The evidence in regard to the ability of pupils to supplement the text is stronger than it is regarding the factors already considered. In test A of the first series for the sixth grade, the pupils used geographies, books of reference, and maps, and some wrote that they tried to imagine the map of Africa which they had previously studied, and tried to see the location of the places mentioned.

In the second series, in the corresponding test, the pupils showed by their questions, and by the citation of facts already known about the Puritans, that they were adding to the text placed before them or that they were tending to do so.

The seventh grades supplemented in similar ways, i. e., by naming books to which they had referred, by giving additional facts, and by asking questions which showed that they were reaching out beyond the lesson.

A few teachers stated in these reports on test A of the first series, that not all of the pupils who said they had used books, had really done so. On the other hand, one class, at least, that usually made frequent use of references did not do so in connection with this test. The reports of many of the pupils contained evidence of outside reading, so that a large part of the children must have made use of references in the preparation of the test. In the first series 173, or 20.5%, supplemented the text, or reported that they had done so. In the second series, 269, or 31.8%, gave evidence of having done so. These numbers would be considerably increased by adding those who said they would refer to other books, or in some other way add to the statements given.

In test E, the supplementing is shown by the questioning in response to the sixth question of the test. In making the tabulation, all questions not relevant to the lesson were included under the heading, " Did not understand." If, then, from the total number of questions asked in each test, the number of questions answered in the text be subtracted, we have left the number of questions which tend to further the pupils' understanding and knowledge of the texts given. The results thus obtained show that in test E of the first series, 454 supplementary questions were asked, and that 597 were asked in the corresponding test of the second series. Part of these questions were about the meanings of words, part about facts, and part about reasons, the fact questions largely predominating. In the first series, 45 pupils asked about the meanings of words; in the second test 33 asked similar questions. Questions about facts were asked by 251 pupils in the first test, and by 294 in the second. Reasons were called for by 145 pupils in the first test, and by 104 in the second. Thus not only the number of the questions, but their nature as well, and the number of pupils asking them show that pupils possess the ability to supplement the text given them for study.

*Nature of some of the questions asked.*

Some of the questions are of great value. Many children asked what *rosin* and *naval stores* are. They asked for the location of Atlanta, and wanted to know why and how Atlanta was destroyed. They asked if Atlanta and Savannah are on the Fall Line, and wanted to know how Savannah could have so deep a harbor when it is so far from the coast. They inquired whether the coal and iron mines, which the text says are in the north, are in the northern part of Georgia, or in the Northern states. Why has Atlanta grown rapidly? How can Georgia manufacture so much with such poor harbors? How do they get the rosin and turpentine? All these are questions asked by sixth grade pupils writing test E in the second series. In the lesson about the races, given to the seventh grades, some of the questions asked were: Who are the people along the Kongo? How do they live? Where is the original home of the white race? Why did some of the people migrate into other countries and others stay in their own country? Why don't the mountains of our country separate any races of people? Who came to know about these different races of people? Why do the races differ from each other? In the lesson about India, some of the questions asked by the seventh grade were as follows: What are Aryan people and what are jute goods? In what part of India is the manu-facturing? What right has the British government to rule over India? Could the people of India do more for themselves if so disposed? If the British government didn't have control over India, would it get along as well?

*Indefiniteness in questioning.*

Many more questions were intended which were not expressed as questions. In the first series, 288 pupils, or 34.8%, indicated subjects about which they would like to ask questions, but did not ask the questions. Sometimes they simply gave topics, and it was not clear what the question was intended to bring out about the topics. In the second test, 243 pupils, or 29.3%, were so lacking in clearness that the questions were not understood. It is evident, however, that many pupils in these grades can ask questions, and questions of value. Other pupils need training in clear expression so that they may be more exact in their questioning. As it is, they merely hint as to the direction in which their thoughts tend.

Further evidence of the ability of children of the grades tested to add relevant matter to the text given is seen in the answers to the fifth question in test E. This question reads: What further facts do you know about any of these topics? In the first test, about 28% of the pupils gave facts that were relevant; in the second test the number who gave related facts was a little more than 29% of the whole number. A very few pupils gave irrele-vant matter, and more than one-third in each test gave facts from the text used in the test. The latter probably misunderstood the question.

*The ability to see problems relating to the lesson.*

That children in the sixth and seventh grades can see prob-lems related to the subject which they are studying is shown by the questions quoted above in the discussion of the sixth ques-tion in test E. Their ability to sense the author's problems is revealed in a curious way. In writing test A, a number of pupils began to write a list of the important facts or topics in the les-son, and gradually changed their statements to questions, indi-cating that they had confused the statement of facts with the questions which called for them. They were feeling the author's questions or problems which had brought about the statements in the text. The following paper, given *verbatim*, illustrates this tendency:

" When studing I put down the chief parts, as follows: When they settled. What goods they imported. What we see know from olden generations. What the settlers began to do. What aded the manufacturing and industry. What sprang up along the coasts. In time what did New England become. What are the most important goods. What did the waterfalls do too help manufacturing. On what chief thing did New England became a great country."

In some papers, statements or topics only were given. In others, there were questions only; but a good many were of the mixed type shown above.

The questions asked in the two kinds of tests, A and E, indicate strongly that pupils can feel the author's problem, and can see problems growing out of the lesson presented, i. e., supplementary problems.

### Grouping related ideas.

In test A of the second series, 12 pupils in a certain seventh grade said that, in studying the lesson, they had grouped related ideas together. Six others in the same grade said that they would do so. Five pupils in the sixth grade representing four different classes said they would group related ideas in studying the lesson assigned. As no pupil actually put any of this work on his paper, the ability of these pupils in this direction cannot be estimated. All that can be said is that at least 23 pupils of the whole number whose papers were counted had some idea of grouping together ideas which are related in some way.

### What test C required.

Test C differs radically from tests A and E in nature. In the two latter, the text was given and the pupils were required to find the problem, if any problem was found. In test C, however, only the problem was given and the pupils were to show how they would solve it.

*How the pupils proposed to solve the problems.*

In examining Table II,[1] which gives the results of this test, it is noticed that very few children wrote facts or questions, possibly because the text was not before their eyes to suggest either procedure. The things which they did most frequently were to give the topics which they would try to study, and to tell the sources to which they would go for information. In the first series 539, or 61.3%, of the pupils indicated the sources to which they would go for information; in the second series 473, or 53.8%, did so. These numbers do not include those who said they would ask teachers, parents, or other people for the facts needed to answer the questions.

*Sources of information named by the pupils.*

The sources named by the pupils of the sixth grade include geography textbooks, supplementary geographies, maps, encyclopedias, histories, newspapers, the library, the almanac, and the dictionary, most of these being given repeatedly. One child suggested asking a man from Pittsburg why that city had become so important; and another said he would ask the cigar dealer why tobacco is now grown extensively in the North.

The first and second series of test C for the seventh grade are very different and while not furnishing a good basis for comparison of results, served to show whether the pupils were thinking of what they were doing, or were working mechanically. In the first series, this grade gave about the same references as the sixth, but gave magazines instead of the almanac. One pupil suggested writing to an editor to find the answer.

In the second series, most pupils said they would read papers, or magazines, or letters about the candidates for office, and would look up the records of the men. Six said they would use the history, geography, encyclopedia, or dictionary in answering the question. They did not mention what they expected to find about the candidates in these books. Several of these seventh grade pupils gave answers which showed good thinking. They would listen to people talking, would hear lectures and speeches; would try to see the candidates and ask them questions; they would try to get acquainted with friends of the candidates and learn about the latter from them; or they would

---

[1]See Appendix.

4

write to the newspapers. While a very few declared boldly that they would vote for the candidate of the party to which they belonged and would work for his election, many pupils said they would investigate the private and political life of the candidates, and would vote for the best man. The following paper, written by a boy, is typical of a good many of the papers written:

" I would first see which one seemed to be the best one to govern. I would find out all about their characters personally. Then I would see if they were able to do their business. I would then size them up very close, and then vote for the one I thought was the most fit for the office."

About one-sixth of the whole number who wrote this test expressed themselves in such a way that it seemed as if they intended to find out about one candidate only.

This test about the selection of a candidate, test C of the second series for the seventh grade, gave more opportunities for originality and independent procedure than the others, since it was decidedly out of the beaten track of the rest of the work. Though only about one-third of the pupils writing this test gave answers which were considered adequate, many more showed intelligent, original efforts as far as they went. Unfortunately they stopped short of fulfilling the requirement of the question.

## The formulation of hypotheses by pupils.

An unexpected result of this test was the manifestation of the ability of the pupils to form hypotheses as a basis for solving the problem presented to them. More than a score of children in each of the two grades volunteered explanations which were quite relevant. This was especially noticeable in the sixth grade test about tobacco growing in the North, and in the seventh grade test about famines in India.

Some of the explanations given by the sixth grade are as follows: 1. Change in climate either in the South or in the North. 2. South needs land for cotton. 3. Better facilities for manufacture and transportation in the North. 4. Cheaper to grow tobacco in the North than to have it shipped from the South. 5. Increased demand for tobacco. 6. Changes in economic conditions in the South due to the Civil War. 7. People of the

North have learned how to cultivate tobacco. 8. Possibly a better quality can be grown in the North than in the South.

In regard to the frequent famines in India, the seventh grade pupils hazarded the hypotheses that they might be due to climatic conditions, to the nature of the surface, to poor soil, to unfavorable winds, to inability to obtain sufficient water for irrigation, to occasional floods, to some insect which destroyed the crops, to oppressive government like that of Turkey, to density of population, to lack of knowledge of farming, to indolence, to lack of foresight or thrift, or to lack of adequate means for transportation and communication.

Not all the theories advanced were as relevant or sensible as those just given; but the fact that so many were given is indicative of the ability of children in these grades to form hypotheses which are worth considering as possible explanations of the problems demanding solution.

*Summary.*

On the whole, the three different kinds of tests in geography given pupils in the sixth and seventh grades show that these pupils can employ the various factors of higher or logical study to a considerable extent. They were evidently not conscious of the steps in systematic study; yet supplementing their account of what they had done or would do in study by the results produced when they were called upon to employ the various factors, a sufficiently large number gave evidence of their use to warrant the conclusion that these pupils can find the subject or leading thought of a lesson; they can organize the material presented; they can supplement the textbook intelligently; they can ask intelligent questions involving valuable problems; and they can to some extent formulate sensible hypotheses for the solution of problems. The ability to work in characteristic ways is shown by the sources employed for information, by the theories advanced, by the questions asked, and, to a lesser degree, in various other ways.

# CHAPTER V

## ARE PUPILS BEING TAUGHT TO STUDY SYSTEMATICALLY IN THE ELEMENTARY SCHOOLS

*The waste of effort shown by the tests.*

In the preceding chapter it was shown that a sufficiently large number of pupils in the grades tested employed the steps of logical study to warrant the conclusion that it is within the power of pupils of at least the sixth and seventh grades to make use of them. Aside, however, from the indefiniteness of the language employed, which often quite concealed the pupils' meaning, Tables I, II, and III reveal the fact that there is great waste in studying. In test A of the first series, 14% described their procedure in studying in indefinite terms, saying they would "think," "study," "try to understand." About 38% of the pupils thought the thing to do was to write a more or less literal version of the text, and about 29% memorized the text to some extent. Nearly one-fifth of the whole number showed that they did not know what to do either by doing nothing at all or doing something not required. These figures show that a good deal of effort was undirected, and that much was misdirected. The pupils wavered between indefiniteness, and mechanical study. They did not clearly know the right things to do, and there was a great scattering of effort in various fruitless kinds of work.

Table II shows a very high per cent. of those whose ideas were so indefinitely expressed that the meaning could not be determined. It shows, also, great expenditure of effort in unnecessary ways. While about one-third of the pupils showed by their answers that they could take adequate measures to solve the problem given, thus indicating that it is possible for pupils of the age of these to do such work, the question is: What about the two-thirds whose work was not adequate? Some solutions were distinctly inadequate, from about one-fourth to one-third, and the rest of the papers were so indefinite that no judgment could be formed as to their worth in this particular.

Table III reveals a still greater degree of inefficiency than either of the other two. In test E of the first series, more than

50% of the pupils failed to find the main thought in an ordinary geography lesson; in the corresponding test of the second series, more than 75% failed to find it. More than two-thirds in each test failed to make an adequate list of the principal topics, though the matter presented was simple enough so that some pupils made excellent lists. The greatest difficulty experienced by the pupils was in connection with the requirements to find the most important thing in the lesson, and to give reasons for thinking it so important. An appreciable per cent. chose a minor point in the lesson, and several chose something not in the lesson at all. Many named more than one thing as being the most important *thing* in the lesson, some even including practically every point of the lesson. Such answers had to be classified as indefinite. Many gave a topic which was so general, so unlimited, that their answers, too, were marked indefinite. The reasoning gave the poorest results in these tests. It was based frequently upon some personal consideration. A thing was considered most important because it was interesting to the writer; because he had never known it before; because he *had* known it before; because he might need it in his geography lesson; because he might need to talk about it some day. Or, having named several items as being most important, a pupil would then advance reasons for the importance of one of them.

The lack of clearness in expression and the misdirection of mental activity are shown in the responses to the fifth and sixth requirements of test E. In response to the question: What other facts do you know about any of these topics? more than fifty per cent. of the answers in each test were irrelevant, were taken from the text which was being studied, or bore no relation to the requirement.

*Reasons why the factors of logical study are not employed more generally.*

If enough pupils use the various factors of proper study to show that it is possible for children of their age to employ them, the questions arise: Why do not many more of the pupils employ them? Why are they not in common use? In trying to solve this problem, a study was made of the present schoolroom situation by means of visits to some seventy classes, and by a *questionnaire* given to one hundred and sixty-five teachers with the object of trying to find what their ideas in regard to study are, and what they try to have their pupils do when they teach them to study.

This *questionnaire* consisted of six parts and the results are shown in Tables IV to IX inclusive.[1] As far as could be avoided, no clue was given to the teachers writing this *questionnaire* which could in any way influence their answers. The aim was to discover the things which stood out prominently enough in consciousness to secure expression when the process of study was being described or illustrated. Had direct questions been asked about the various factors of study, probably many of the teachers would have felt the influence of suggestion in shaping their replies.

The facts given by teachers when describing how they memorize, are shown in Table IV. It is interesting to note that at least 78% of the teachers read or study a poem or chapter before memorizing it. That is as it should be, since memorizing should be based upon thought relations. But does the studying here referred to consist of the tracing or establishing of such relations? Further along in the same table, we see that only 23.6% of the teachers report that they divide a selection into thought units in memorizing, while a much larger number use such mechanical divisions as lines, sentences, or stanzas. Again, only about 11% reported that they pictured situations, i. e., imagined; 13% said they traced thought relations; and less than 6% that they associated the ideas of the poem or chapter with known facts. More than one-fourth reported that in memorizing they use cumulative repetition, i. e., the House-that-Jack-built order of procedure, going from line to line, then back again to the beginning for a fresh start. Wherever details are given explicitly enough to make the meaning clear, the mechanical side is seen to predominate.

Some explanation may be needed for the heading in regard to the use of mechanical aids in memorizing. The people here listed depend upon the rhyme, the rhythm, the first words in successive lines, and other mechanical devices in committing to memory, rather than upon the sequence of ideas. It would be interesting to test how the ease with which the people who memorize by thought units compares with the effort required by those

---

[1] See Appendix.

who depend upon the mechanical aspects alone in committing to memory. An expression might have been obtained from the two classes of people as to whether they find memorizing easy or difficult. Such statements would have value in connection with this report.

Some explanation of the failure of so many pupils to work systematically and effectively may be seen in the fact that in stating the various things which they think ought to be done in " thinking about a lesson " (see Table V), not more than 33⅓% of the teachers agreed upon any one item. There were at least twenty things mentioned which should be done, and the element considered most important was indicated by one-third of the writers. This was, " Find the important points "—a very necessary thing to do in studying, the strange part being that so few of the teachers felt its importance. A number of the other items given are either so general as to give no idea of what the writers really meant, or they are mechanical, e. g., apperceive, reason, understand the meaning, memorize. Only 15% felt keenly enough to mention it the necessity of finding the main thought or problem. The questions arise : If teachers do not feel the necessity of finding the problem sufficiently to speak of it in describing the process of study, will they be likely to think of it when working with pupils? Will not this lack in teachers account for the failure of so many pupils to find the problem or leading thought of the lessons given them for study? If not more than 15% of the teachers mention it, could one expect more than 5% of the pupils to do so? (Between four and five per cent. of the pupils who wrote test A, spoke of finding the subject or principal thought of the lesson.)

If the corresponding items in Tables V and VI be added so as to get the ideas of the teachers who told what ought to be done in " thinking about a lesson," and of those who expressed their views as to what else should be done in studying a lesson, the factor advocated by the greatest number is mentioned by only 52% of the writers. The twenty-six other items occurring in the tables are advocated by numbers ranging from nearly 39%, who spoke of understanding the lesson, down to about 1%, who mentioned the need of drill to form habits.

*Lack of clearness as to the process of studying.*

It is interesting to note how long a list of mental activities is given by the teachers in Tables V and VI. Attention, interest, perception, apperception, imagination, memory, correlation, comparison, and reason—these make up one-third of the separate items of these two tables, and tell a minimum as to what is really to be done. The large number of items, the indefiniteness of many of them, and the scattered per cents. show that these teachers do not clearly see the nature of study. No steps stand out strongly in the minds of a large number, but instead there is confusion of thought, and lack of agreement.

The teachers who wrote this *questionnaire* were, for the most part, a selected proup,—for college students are usually so regarded, and eighty-two per cent. were students in Teachers Colege. With very few exceptions all were experienced teachers, and all but twenty-six had taught in elementary schools. If these teachers, with their experience and advanced training, are as indefinite in their ideas about the process of studying as tables V and VI show them to be, the ideas of other teachers could hardly be expected to be more definite and practical.

In answering the questions: Do you do any of the things mentioned under 1, 2, and 3, more frequently than the others? If so, which are they? the teachers limited the number of steps mentioned but still scattered their votes, showing the same failure to recognize essential features. Twenty-four per cent., the highest number in the table, said they memorized more frequently than anything else; and as low a per cent. as appears, 1.2%, represents the number who recognized the importance of finding the aim or problem. One of the highest numbers in Table I, which shows the pupils' report of how they study, represents those who memorize to some extent; and one of the low numbers, though not the lowest, represents those who tried to find the principal thought or idea of the lesson—that which in Table VII corresponds to the aim or problem. A larger percentage of pupils than of teachers spoke of finding the main thought, of finding the important points in a lesson, and of supplementing the text.

The fifth question answered by the teachers was: When you were a pupil in the elementary school, were you taught to use any of these steps or processes systematically? If so, which ones? The listed answers are shown in Table VIII.[1] Eliminating those who reported definitely that they were not taught, those who did not remember, and those whose answers were not relevant—nearly 65% of the teachers, there are 35% left who say they were systematically taught. 20.6%, much more than half of this remnant, were taught to memorize, while the factors of logical study are hardly recognized at all in this report.

As might be expected from the preceding report, the answers to the sixth question added little or nothing to the impression already made by the teachers. This question reads: If you have taught in an elementary school, have you ever trained your pupils there to use any of these steps or processes? If you have, which steps or processes were they? Eleven teachers, or 6.7% of the whole, frankly said *no* in answer to the question.

The various factors of logical study appear in the answers to the sixth question (see Table IX),[2] but the numbers who say that they taught them are insignificant. The largest number taught their pupils to " understand the thought," whatever they may have meant by that; and teaching pupils to memorize appears second in the list. However, not more than approximately one-third of the writers had taught any one factor out of the entire list of twenty-eight items.

### Summary of results of teachers' questionnaire.

The *questionnaire* as a whole reveals that these teachers themselves are lacking the proper conception of the process of higher study; that they tend to exalt memorizing; and that they do not as a class accord recognition to any factor or factors as being essential to study. In several instances, the factors which they have recognized to a considerable extent, were employed largely by the pupils in their studies; and the factors which the teachers have overlooked in their reports were used but little by the pupils in their tests.

### A second means of investigating present procedure in teaching children to study.

With the purpose of investigating still further the extent to which pupils are being taught to study in the higher sense of

---

[1] See Appendix.
[2] See Appendix.

the word, seventy recitations were observed in various cities of
the United States. During the year of 1905-06 a *questionnaire*
was sent out to a number of principals of schools.[1] This *questionnaire* was to be filled out by the principals after certain recitations had been observed. While information was desired mainly
in regard to how the teachers treated the thought-content of the
lesson in the assignment, what she expected the pupils to do with
it in preparing the lesson, and how she disposed of it during
the recitation period, the other items were added, not only to
supplement the chief purpose, but also that they might prevent
the main points from being so prominent that the report upon
them would be more or less biased.

At the time that this *questionnaire* was sent out, the writer
was doing some experimental work with a fourth grade class in
reading; consequently, the principals were asked to observe reading classes in the intermediate department, including fourth,
fifth and sixth grades. Reports were received from Duluth,
Minn.; Madison, Wis.; Passaic, N. J.; and Baltimore, Md. The
writer visited a number of schools, both public and private, in
New York City, and several classes in the public schools of
Passaic, N. J. The subjects in which recitations were observed
were reading, history, arithmetic, geography and language.

The data obtained are tabulated according to subjects, and
while there is much that is valuable in a recitation which is not
susceptible of tabulation, for example, the spirit of the teacher,
and the classroom atmosphere, still it is worth while to note
some of the things done or left undone in the way of training
pupils to work independently and logically.

*Observations of recitations in reading.*

Twenty-nine reading lessons were observed in nineteen classes
from the third to the eighth grade inclusive, excepting the seventh grade. The facts in regard to the assignments and recitations are shown separately and are given in the accompanying
classifications:

---

[1]See Appendix.

## ASSIGNMENT OF READING LESSONS.

| | Classes. | Per ct. |
|---|---|---|
| 1. Total number .......................... | 29 | |
| 2. No assignment made..................... | 2 | 6.9 |
| 3. Assignment not observed................. | 6 | 20.7 |
| 4. Assignment of words to be studied......... | 16 | 55.2 |
| 5. Formal assignment (pages, paragraphs, or title of lesson indicated)............... | 15 | 51.7 |
| 6. Pupils told to prepare to give thought in their own words .......................... | 6 | 20.7 |
| 7. Lesson discussed before class study........ | 5 | 17.2 |
| 8. Teacher assigned questions to be answered.. | 3 | 10.3 |
| 9. Pupils instructed to find topics or headings.. | 3 | 10.3 |
| 10. Allusions discussed or assigned........... | 2 | 6.9 |
| 11. Pupils directed to prepare to read lesson smoothly ... ........................... | 2 | 6.9 |
| 12. Class directed to find beautiful language.... | 1 | 3.4 |

## RECITATIONS OF READING LESSONS.

| | Recitations. | Per ct. |
|---|---|---|
| 1. Lessons observed . .................... | 29 | |
| 2. Oral reading (not based on study of thought in class)..................in | 24 | 82.7 |
| 3. Class supplemented (explained, imagined, questioned, referred to other articles), in | 16 | 55.2 |
| 4. Teacher asked questions............... " | 15 | 51.7 |
| 5. Words studied ..................... " | 12 | 41.4 |
| 6. Lesson reproduced orally.............. " | 6 | 20.7 |
| 7. Class exercised initiative.............. " | 9 | 31. |
| 8. Class discussion ..................... " | 5 | 17.2 |
| 9. Oral reading (based on study of thought in class) . ........................in | 3 | 10.3 |
| 10. Children made outline of lesson........ " | 2 | 6.9 |

*Nature of the lesson assignments in the classes in reading.*

A fact not shown by these classifications is that in more than fifty per cent. of the classes observed, the entire assignment consisted of giving the class a certain number of pages to read, giving out a lesson by its title, and either drilling upon words or else assigning word-study as part of the lesson. There was no preparation in these classes, no development or statement of an aim, and no directions whatever as to the treatment of the thought of the lesson.

In about 7% of the classes no assignment was made at all, the pupils reading at sight; and in about 20% of the classes, no assignment was observed. In about 17% of the classes, there was a talk about the lesson preparatory to its assignment, but this talk did not prepare for independent and systematic study of the lesson. No aim was put before the pupils which required any use of the thought contained in the lessons and the pupils were left to a more or less desultory reading of the story. These lessons were not even assigned for the sake of the language, since not one of the teachers called attention to the form in which the thought was expressed. It is a matter of interest to know whether teachers who make such assignments can give a good reason why they teach reading in their classes.

In a third grade, the pupils were told to find a good subject or name for a certain story which they were to read. In an eighth grade, after a preliminary study of Washington's *Farewell Address,* the teacher told the class to " Find what points Washington gives for unity." In these two classes only did the preliminary work send the pupils to their study with an aim to be accomplished through mastery of the thought of the lesson. Only these pupils were required to organize material, and select or reject ideas according to the purpose to be accomplished.

Only 10% of the teachers assigned questions to be answered. No report was made as to the nature of the questions in two lessons. In the third lesson, the questions dealt with the thought of successive sentences without any differentiation of values, and therefore gave no aid in teaching pupils to study discriminatingly and independently.

*Summary of assignments.*

To sum up the assignments briefly, in but three of the recitations observed, that is in about 10% of the whole number of reading lessons observed, were the classes given such a preparation for the study of the lesson that the pupils could go to their work intelligently, and with the prospect of doing effective studying. For the most part, the work was desultory or formal, and led nowhere in particular. It contributed nothing to the formation of right habits of study in the pupils belonging to the classes, save in the two classes specially mentioned where the pupils were to find a subject, or were to organize the material of the lesson. This neglect of thoughtful assignments was not due to lack of thoughtful material upon which to work. The subject matter employed included *The Great Stone Face, Evangeline, King Philip, Shakspeare,* and *The English Slave Boys in Rome,* and other good selections for study, but all were equally neglected.

### The recitations in reading.

Turning to the tabulated results of the observations of the recitation periods of these reading classes, we see that approximately 82% of the classes read orally without previous attention to the thought of the lesson in the recitation period. In not one of these instances had the thought been studied in the assignment of the lesson, so that these twenty-four lessons contributed nothing to the gaining of knowledge or skill in the use of right ways of mastering thought.

### Questioning in the reading recitations.

In more than 50% of the recitations, the teacher asked questions, while the pupils questioned in less than one-seventh of the classes,—surely not a general display of initiative on the part of the pupils; though, as has been shown in chapter IV, pupils can ask excellent questions. The teachers' questions, moreover, dealt with small points to a great extent. In but three recitations could they be considered large, and what might be called thought-provoking. " Why was Shakespeare considered great?" " What is the main thought of the paragraph you have read?" These were among the strong questions asked. For the most part the teachers asked about words and phrases, and isolated, unimportant facts and thoughts selected here and there from the lessons. These questions did not require comparison, selection, grouping, or testing to any great degree save in the three classes just cited.

### Supplementary material in the reading classes.

No attempt was made in these recitations to guide the interests of the children, or to give them any training in seeking

and using supplementary material. No books were used save
the reading books containing the lessons assigned, and no individual reference work was given to any pupil. There was thus
little opportunity to judge of the relevancy and reliability of additional data, and no training whatever in finding and arranging
material bearing upon the lesson.

### The study of words.

In 41% of the recitations, words were studied, but only one
class attempted to find the meanings of puzzling words by the
use of the context. In a few instances, pupils tried to find the
meaning of the word they needed by using another in its place.
These pupils had a good basis for judging of the value of the
meaning when found and were learning to be independent.

### The exercise of initiative in reading classes.

In the five recitations in which class discussion took place, the
pupils talked freely about points in the story, criticized each
other's recitations, checked any tendency to wander from the
point, decided upon the place in a story where dramatization
might well begin, and, in general, added greatly to the value of
the work in hand, besides gaining practice in seeing and solving
difficulties in reading, and in estimating the relevancy and worth
of their own recitations. All this work involved initiative on the
part of the pupils and it is in place here to mention other mani-
festations of this trait in the recitations observed. In the classes
where it was permitted or encouraged, pupils asked for meanings of words which they needed; also, for explanations of statements. They even questioned the statements of the text, and corrected the recitations of their mates. They not only held each
other to the point under discussion, but were ready to render
needed assistance in mastering words and thoughts. They asked
readers to "speak louder," and took different seats so as to
hear better. Discussion, questioning by pupils, and other forms
of initiative were seen in nine classes, or 31%, of all the classes
observed.

### Summary of observations of recitations in reading.

In summing up these observations, it may be said that only
two teachers of the whole number visited seemed to have definite

ideas about training the pupils in right ways of studying. In all other classes, there was but little done to give the pupils such training and that little was apparently incidental rather than definitely anticipated.

*Observations of classes in history.*

Five lesson assignments in sixth grade history were observed, and three recitations, the two exercises being separated in time. The results can be shown briefly.

|  |  | Classes. | Per ct |
|---|---|---|---|
| 1. | Total number of classes observed................... | 5 |  |
| 2. | Lesson assigned by subject.................. | 4 | 80 |
| 3. | Lesson assigned by pages or paragraphs...... | 2 | 40 |
| 4. | Pupils directed to references................. | 1 | 20 |
| 5. | Pupils directed to ask questions.............. | 1 | 20 |
| 6. | Pupils directed to read lesson............... | 1 | 20 |
| 7. | Pupils directed to read smoothly............ | 1 | 20 |

*The recitations in history.*

Only one of the five teachers observed conducted the recitation period in such a way as to exercise the pupils in logical study. Her pupils chose the title for the lesson, which they had been reading not only in the school texts but in references obtained from the city library. They dictated an outline of the lesson to the teacher which the latter wrote on the board. They criticized each other's selection of subject, and the arrangement of topics. After a lively oral recitation, they wrote a vigorous account of the subject discussed, following the outline which they had made. There was good work done in good spirit, and in a systematic way. None of the other recitations included any work of this nature, but were rather a re-rendering of the book narrative. One class dramatized the lesson successfully.

*Observations of classes in arithmetic.*

Fourteen arithmetic classes were visited, though in eight of them no assignment was seen as the practice seemed to be to make the assignment at some separate period. Of the six assignments observed, three were entirely formal, three required pupils to form problems, and in two cases individual assignments were made to certain pupils.

Thirteen recitations were observed, of which 69% were formal drill exercises. In 77% of the classes, the teacher asked all questions and in 69% of them, she gave all the problems. In five classes, the teacher developed a new topic, but in only two of these classes did the pupils question. But two classes, or about 15% of all observed, attempted to form problems. In but one class did the pupils correct the errors made by the class, and only one class prepared an outline of the topic studied. The teachers were, as a rule, the very prominent centres of all the work, and the pupils exercised but little initiative, and did next to nothing in the way of systematic, independent mastery of the topics included in their arithmetic.

*Observations of classes in geography.*

The geography observations were of special interest, since geography was the subject used for the tests. Fifteen classes were observed, twelve of them being classes which had written the tests. Only the observations upon these twelve are reported, so as to show whether the class procedure throws light upon the work done in tests. In the assignments, the following are the facts:

|  |  | Classes. | Per ct. |
|---|---|---|---|
| 1. | Total classes visited.......................... | 12 |  |
| 2. | Number of assignments not observed....... | 7 | 58.3 |
| 3. | Number of assignments by pages........... | 2 | 16.7 |
| 4. | Number of assignments by subject......... | 2 | 16.7 |
| 5. | Number of times teacher gave questions..... | 1 | 8.3 |

The recitations showed these details:

|  |  | Classes. | Per ct. |
|---|---|---|---|
| 1. | Total number of classes visited................. | 12 |  |
| 2. | Number of drill or review exercises....... | 4 | 33.3 |
| 3. | Number of times teacher gave outline...... | 3 | 25. |
| 4. | Number of times pupils found topics....... | 1 | 8.3 |
| 5. | Number of memory recitations observed.... | 1 | 8.3 |
| 6. | Number of times teacher supplemented text. | 1 | 8.3 |
| 7. | Number of times pupils supplemented text.. | 1 | 8.3 |
| 8. | Number of times pupils reasoned or explained | 5 | 41.7 |
| 9. | Number of times teacher questioned....... | 9 | 75. |
| 10. | Number of recitations not observed........ | 2 | 16.7 |

*Summary of observations of classes in geography.*

These observations, like most of the others, reveal the teacher doing nearly all of the work, and very little initiative or opportunity for independent, constructive work left to the pupils. In not a single class did the pupils question or participate in discussion. It is hardly possible that not one of the classes observed was studying subject matter interesting enough to suggest some problem to the pupils, or to be worthy of class consideration. In but one class did the pupils organize the material of the lesson, and in only one did they add anything to the text. The factors of logical study were almost totally lacking in all these classes, though the subject studied is full of opportunities for their employment. The *résumé* of visits is a strong indication of the reason why the classes writing tests made so little display of any knowledge of the steps in logical study.

*Observations of recitations in language.*

The remaining observations were made in classes where language was being studied. The subject was formal, and gave little opportunity for logical study. It was rather an exercise in correct forms, and in the formation of taste. However, the assignments and recitations are hereby summarized:

### OBSERVATIONS OF LANGUAGE LESSONS.

| | Classes. | Per ct. |
|---|---|---|
| 1. Number of classes observed..................... | | 7 |
| 2. Number of assignments not observed....... | 4 | 55.6 |
| 3. Selection assigned for study.............. | 3 | 42.9 |
| 4. Teacher gave questions to be studied........ | 1 | 14.3 |
| 5. Teacher and pupils prepared an outline...... | 1 | 14.3 |
| 6. Pupils required to write composition........ | 1 | 14.3 |
| 7. Preliminary class work................... | 1 | 14.3 |

### RECITATION OF LANGUAGE LESSONS.

| | Classes. | Per ct. |
|---|---|---|
| 1. Recitations not observed................. | 1 | 14.3 |
| 2. Oral or written reproduction............. | 2 | 28.6 |
| 3. Review ..................................... | 1 | 14.3 |
| 4. Written composition ................... | 1 | 14.3 |
| 5. Sentential analysis ..................... | 1 | 14.3 |

5

|  | Classes. | Per ct. |
|---|---|---|
| 6. Class discussion and criticism............. | 4 | 55.6 |
| 7. All questions asked by teacher............. | 3 | 42.9 |
| 8. Pupils questioned . ...................... | I | 14.3 |
| 9. Pupils explained or gave reasons.......... | 2 | 28.6 |
| 10. Teacher gave outlines.................... | I | 14.3 |
| 11. Pupils prepared outlines................. | I | 14.3 |

Some of the freest, strongest work seen in all the classes visited was in connection with two of these language classes. One class of boys argued *pro* and *con* with a will in regard to some point in technical grammar, and the teacher was wise enough to keep them to the point and leave them free to work out their problem. In one class in written composition, there was hearty co-operation on the part of the pupils in preparing the *résumé* of the material which was to serve as a guide in writing. There was free and friendly criticism of pupils' work by other pupils, and suggestions of value were offered. This teacher, too, was wise enough to direct the efforts and keep the class working profitably while working freely.

*Summary of questionnaire and observations.*

In completing this chapter, in which have been discussed the pupils' great need of knowing how to study, the teachers' ideals of proper study, and the observations of recitations, the conclusion is forced upon us that, although pupils possess ability to employ the various factors of proper study, the teachers lack a clear conception of what such study is. The teachers who wrote the *questionnaire* do not themselves employ these factors to any great extent; and the teachers observed in the class rooms are not training their pupils to use them. The teacher is the center and moving power in nearly all of the work, and the requirements laid upon the pupils involve mechanical effort to a large degree. The aim of the work as a whole seems to be the mastery of subject matter; the development of the power to work independently, intelligently, and economically is almost entirely ignored. The teachers do not know of what such study consists and consequently give little thought to its cultivation. They would probably do so if they had definite ideas as to its nature, for they are frequently heard to lament the fact that their pupils do not know how to study, or to think.

# CHAPTER VI

## CAN PUPILS IN THE ELEMENTARY SCHOOL BE TAUGHT TO STUDY SYSTEMATICALLY

*The attempt to train pupils in the use of the factors of logical study.*

In Chapter IV the statement was made that part of the classes tested in both the sixth and seventh grades were trained in the use of the factors of higher study between the first and second series of tests, the idea being to discover what difference such training would produce in the results of the second series. It must be stated frankly that the conditions governing this attempted training were far from ideal. Two of the five classes trained in the sixth grade, and three of the four classes trained in the seventh grade were in schools of practice where the pupils were not under the care of one teacher continuously; but were taught by pupil teachers or special teachers part of the time. Under such circumstances, the influence and training of even a strong teacher, would not have full opportunity to produce their effect, and not all of these teachers were strong, either in their mental grasp or their teaching ability. At least two were very weak.

Then, too, with but one exception, not one of the teachers of these classes had attended the lectures in which Professor McMurry advanced the theory of systematic study, so that they lacked both the lectures, and the accompanying discussions of them by experienced teachers. They were taught the theory of study at second hand by those who had attended this class, and an interval of three months was a short period for them to learn the theory and then apply it to classes with sufficient success to produce marked results.

To add to the difficulty, there was almost no literature on the subject to put into their hands to help them in understanding the theory and its requirements, and there were no schools practising the theory which could be observed and used as guides. A copy of a paper read by Professor F. M. McMurry before the Department of Superintendence of the National Educational

Association in Louisville, Ky., in March, 1906, on the subject, " Some suggestions for the improvement of the study period," was sent to each teacher who undertook the training work. In addition, a copy was sent of the theoretical discussion of the steps in systematic study which was part of an essay on " The study of the reading lesson in the fourth grade," submitted by the writer in partial fulfillment of the requirements for the degree of Master of Arts in the Faculty of Philosophy, Columbia University, in May, 1906.

Under the compulsion of circumstances the work of training was undertaken even with such adverse conditions, and the courage and good will of the school teachers and school principals who aided in the task are gratefully recognized.

If the training of the pupils was successful, the percentage of pupils in the trained classes who used the factors of logical study in writing the second series ought to be greater than the percentage who used them in the first series; and the number of trained pupils who wrote indefinite, general, or irrelevant answers should be lower in the second series than in the first. An examination of the results of test A, given in Table I of the Appendix, shows that the changes are not always in the direction of greater proficiency for the trained classes, though even under adverse conditions, they excelled in a number of particulars.

Of the answers which are sufficiently definite to show what the pupils did in studying, those which approach nearest to higher study are in regard to finding the subject, finding the important points, verifying the statements, and supplementing the lesson.

*Comparison of grades in regard to finding the subject.*

In the first series, 1.3% of the pupils in the untrained sixth grades spoke of finding the subject. In the second series, 3.1% of them spoke of it. The corresponding per cents. for the trained sixth grades were 0%, and 0.9%. These results have little significance. The pupils of the untrained seventh grades attained 5.4% and 0.9% in the two tests, while the trained seventh grades scored 3.5% and 20% in them. These results show a decided contrast which greatly favors the grades which were trained. The seventh grades not trained made a decided loss, while the trained grades gained 16.5%.

*Organization of the subject matter.*

The results in regard to finding the important points, or organizing the subject matter, are even more favorable to the classes which were trained. The per cents. made by the untrained sixth grades were 9.6% and 24.8% for the first and second series. The trained sixth grades scored only 3.6% in the first series, but rose to 20.7% in the second one—a greater gain both relatively and absolutely than the gain made by the other group. The untrained seventh grades made 31.8% in the first series, but went down to 21% in the second. The trained classes, on the contrary, went from 21.2% in the first series to 55.3% in the second, a gain of 34.1%—a very significant advance.

*Verification of statements.*

There were not enough instances of verification of the statements of the text to make the comparison of results of significance. The gains and losses in this particular can be seen in Table I.

*Supplementing the lesson.*

In supplementing the lesson, the untrained sixth grades went from 30.8% in the first series to 40.8% in the second, making a gain of 10%. The trained classes of the same grade went from 30.6% in the first test to 46% in the second. They made about the same per cent. as the other classes in the first series but made a gain of 16% in the second series, a balance of 6% in their favor over the other classes. In the first series, the untrained seventh grades scored 24.5%; in the second, they scored 64.5%, an absolute gain of 40%. The trained seventh grades recorded 22.3% in the first test, and rose to 51.8%, an absolute gain of 29.5%. They did not nearly equal the untrained grades in this part of their study, though they excelled in their ideas about finding the subject of the lesson, and in finding the important points in a lesson.

In the items which show formality, indefiniteness, or irrelevancy in the pupils' ideas of study, the per cents. do not always stand in favor of the trained classes, but sometimes show a balance against them. Under the headings, " Concentrated attention," " Memorized," " Studied the lesson," and " Answer irrelevant," the results are favorable to both the sixth and seventh grades which were trained. The results under the headings, " Thought: tried to understand," and " Did not understand," are adverse to one of the grades trained, but not to both. The results in regard to writing facts stand to the disadvantage of both trained grades. The other items are either too small in the numbers represented to be of significance, or are of dubious interpretation and may or may not be desirable in proper study. The advantage on the whole, as shown by test A, is with the trained classes.

### The improvement of the classes not trained.

It would have been surprising if the untrained classes had not made improvement in their ways of working during the three months which intervened between the two series of tests, for several of the teachers of these classes were women of great ability as teachers, and were keen enough intellectually to gain much profit from the first series of tests, even though they did not know a second series was to be given later. They saw how helpless many of the pupils were under the requirements of the tests, and saw, also, hints for betterment of conditions. There is also the possibility that some of the pupils may have been roused to better effort by the first tests, though it is much more probable that it was the teacher who profited, and who in turn influenced the procedure of the pupils.

### Comparison of the results of test C.

The results of test C, given in Table II, show no great improvement or advantage for the trained or untrained pupils of either grade. The test in the second series for the seventh grade was so decidedly different in character from the corresponding one in the first series, that in some of the steps of study, comparisons would be unjustifiable. For example, the first test was a book test and called for the use of textbooks. To have used textbooks in the second test would have been out of place. The seventh grades which were trained made a better record than the untrained ones in six of the eleven items of test C. They failed to do as well in four particulars, and made an equal record with them in the increased per cent. of those who said they would ask for information when writing the second series. Unfortunately, the trained seventh grades fell off decidedly in the second test in the adequacy of the steps proposed to solve the problem. Much that the pupils proposed to do was doubtless very good, but it was not sufficient to meet the conditions of the problem. For example, in deciding which candidate to vote for, more than thirty pupils, some trained, some untrained, said they would investigate one candidate. Usually that would be only half enough for the solution of the problem.

In test C, the trained sixth grades gained over the others in seven particulars, including adequacy; fell behind the untrained grades in two factors; and in regard to two items named, i. e., the asking for information and the preparing of questions, the gain or loss is conditioned by other factors. For example, if a pupil did nothing but ask questions and gave no hint as to what he would do with them, his answer could not be considered satisfactory.

The trained sixth grades made a relatively better showing in test C than did the trained seventh grades, and the two grades which had been trained, made a better record on the whole than the untrained ones.

The record was improved sometimes by obtaining a higher per cent. in the second test than in the first, and sometimes the gain in judgment was shown by a lowering of the per cent. in the second trial. For example, a lowering of the per cent. under the heading *Inadequate* meant gain; but under the heading *Adequate* the gain was indicated by an increased per cent. in the second test. When both trained and untrained classes lowered their percentage in the second test, the advantage was considered as belonging to the group which had lowered it to a lesser degree than the other. It might have been that the second test was more difficult than the first one, and in that case, the grade which suffered least because of the increased difficulty was considered the stronger.

*Comparison of the trained and untrained groups in test E.*

A comparison of the relative abilities of the trained and untrained grades as shown by Table III, which contains a statement of the facts given in test E, shows that the trained sixth grades were stronger in their practical work than the untrained sixth grades. They were stronger, also, than the trained seventh grades. Comparisons were made only as to the adequacy of the subjects found, the adequacy of the lists of topics, the ability to find a large topic or thought, the adequacy of the reasons given, the number whose questions called for reasons, and the number whose questions were not clear. Comparisons were not made as to the number who gave relevant facts, because not only ability but knowledge is involved in that report. The trained sixth grades excelled the untrained in keeping near to their first record for adequacy in the subject found, in gain in adequacy of lists, in gain in selecting the large point, in holding nearer to the first record in adequacy of reasoning, in gain in clearness of expression, and in the increased number who asked questions involving reasoning. In the use of all these steps in practical activity in studying, the trained sixth grades as a whole excelled the untrained grades as a whole.

The trained seventh grades excelled the untrained ones in the second test in keeping near their records for finding an adequate subject and for choosing adequate lists of topics; also in the increased number who asked questions involving reasoning about the lesson. The records for the untrained grades are better than for the trained grades in the other activities compared.

*Summary of comparisons of trained and untrained groups.*

The three tests show that on the whole the trained sixth grades made a better record in the second series than the untrained sixth grades. The trained seventh grades excelled the other seventh grades in finding the subject and in selecting the main points of the lesson both in test A and test E, but their record as a whole was not as strong as that of the trained sixth grades. It is doubtful whether, save in the two particulars mentioned, which are both very important, their record was any better than that of the untrained seventh grades.

*An experiment in teaching pupils to study a reading lesson.*

Confirmatory evidence of the ability of pupils in the elementary school to study may be seen in the results obtained from a reading class in the fourth grade in the Speyer School, the school of practice of Teachers College. A series of sixteen lessons was given by the writer to this class in the spring of 1906, to determine whether the pupils of the fourth grade possess the ability to employ the steps in logical study, and whether they can be taught to use them independently and habitually. The lesson periods were from twenty-five to thirty minutes long and there was no study period. The text used for reading was a version of the *Odyssey* edited by Mrs. Lida B. McMurry.

About three weeks before the experiment began, the regular teacher of the grade had begun to give the pupils opportunity to ask questions about the thought of the lesson after it had been read orally. She had tried, also, to have the pupils use synonyms for certain words occurring in the lesson, these being selected by her. The children responded freely in the matter of questioning, but seemed not to feel the need of synonyms and so were not successful with them.

In the first lessons, the teacher (the writer) helped the pupils with difficult words, and proposed the topic or aim for the new lesson. She also tried to secure recognition of the important parts of the lesson in their order by asking the pupils what part of the story they would tell first, what part next, etc., but it was hard work for the pupils. The main points were given slowly and with difficulty, and were poorly worded.

The early recitations showed that the pupils responded with interest to the subject matter, and that they desired information in regard to many things, these frequently being facts which the editor had omitted. They were ready to pass judgment as to character, as for example, when they commended Nausicaa's act of kindness to Ulysses. But these lessons showed, also, that the pupils needed to look for the problems in the story; that they needed training in analysis and organization of the material; in making out the pronunciation and meaning of words, and in thinking out the meaning of sentences. The teacher found, too, that she needed to eliminate herself more thoroughly, and throw more responsibility upon the class.

In the third lesson the pupils were asked to suggest ways for finding out the meaning of words needed in reading. Various means were presented, and at last the class decided to try to use another word in the place of the word not understood. After that lesson, they took care of meanings themselves, asking to have a word substituted for the word which they could not understand. They grew very critical, refusing definitions and explanations, and objecting to words whose substitution did not bring understanding or satisfaction. They would say, " You did not do what I asked you," and more than once a pupil was told to sit down because his answer was not what had been asked for. They were attempting to satisfy needs, and were very discriminating in their judgment about words. The previously felt difficulty about synonyms disappeared whenever the need of such words was felt.

At the same time that the pupils were thrown upon their own responsibility for the meaning of words, ways and means were discussed for pronouncing new words, and that phase of the work was also given over to the class. In regard to phrases and sentences, they decided they could help themselves by reading farther, by trying to think it out, and by asking themselves questions.

The first lesson showed that the pupils were not able to divide the lesson into parts. In the fourth lesson, they were asked to think of a good name for a certain part of the story and to write these names on paper. Out of a class of twenty, one began to write the story, and two or three did nothing. A few were absent. The rest gave the following list, which is a great gain over the first lesson:

> Ulysses meets Nausicaa.
> When Ulysses meets Nausicaa.
> Ulysses and Nausicaa.
> Ulysses speaking to Nausicaa.
> Nausicaa meets the stranger which is Ulysses.
> Ulysses.
> Ulysses gets food and drink.
> Ulysses goes to town.
> Nausicaa clothes Ulysses.

A few others similar to these were given.

Towards the close of the series of lessons, after the pupils had read the booklet of eight pages entitled, *Penelope and Telemachus during Ulysses' Absence,* they were asked to name in order the things they would talk about if they were telling the story to some one at home. They gave the following outline very promptly:

> The princes wish to marry Penelope.
> Penelope deceives the princes.

Telemachus holds a council.
Telemachus goes to inquire about Ulysses.
Telemachus visits Nestor.
Telemachus visits Menelaus.
The suitors making ready to kill Telemachus.
Penelope hears of Telemachus' absence.

Both the nature of the topics and the readiness with which they were given are evidence of gain on the part of the pupils in the ability to discover and express the important thoughts in the subject matter.

*Stating the aim.*

Three booklets were read by the class, namely, *Ulysses among the Phaeacians, Penelope and Telemachus during Ulysses' Absence,* and *Ulysses at Home Again.* When the first booklet was begun, the teacher stated the aim for the book. Before taking up the second booklet, the pupils were asked what questions they might expect to find answered in it. Here are the questions suggested by the class: " What does Ulysses do when he gets home?" " Did he see his wife again?" " Did he have any more troubles?" " Did Penelope and Telemachus have any troubles?" When the third and last booklet was reached, the children were asked what questions they would like to have answered in the rest of the story. They asked so many questions and asked them so rapidly that it was impossible to write them all. " Did Ulysses reach his home safely?" " Did he kill the suitors?" " Did the suitors kill him?" " Did they kill Telemachus?" " Did Penelope marry any of the suitors?" These are some of the questions asked. It is apparent that the teacher did not need to state any aim, since the pupils had furnished such an abundance of them.

*Supplementing the text.*

The lessons showed the readiness of the pupils to supplement the text, to question the meaning, and to form judgments of their own. One example of their filling out and explaining situations was afforded by the answers to the question of a child who asked, " How did Ulysses know that Nausicaa was the daughter of a king? He had never seen her before." The following replies were given: (1) "Because she stayed, although the maidens ran away." (2) "Because she had mules." (3) "Because she had maids." (4) "Maybe she had nice clothes." (5) "Maybe she wore a band of gold on her head." At another time, a child asked, "Why did the suitors want to marry Penelope?" One little girl gave in substance this reply: "Because she was gentle and kind, and was not lazy, but looked after the house. She could spin, and could weave beautiful cloth. She could do her own washing." It was interesting to notice the practical nature of the answer and the fact that the beauty of Penelope was not mentioned as an attraction.

### Forming tentative judgments.

Among other things which the pupils tried to explain in answer to the questions of their mates were the facts that Ulysses asked Nausicaa for *poor* garments; that Alcinous, when sending Ulysses home to Ithaca, put the presents intended for him under the benches of the boat; and that Penelope did not want to marry any of the suitors. One boy thought Ulysses asked for poor clothes with the idea that when he reached the city he could do odd jobs and earn money to buy good clothes. Several had the idea that the reason the gifts were placed under the benches was because the youths convoying Ulysses to Ithaca were dishonest. One girl was quite sure that the reason why Penelope did not choose one of the suitors was because she was afraid of Ulysses. In each case, the pupils were asked how they could probably find out whether their ideas were correct. They said that they might do so by reading more of the story. Each time, as they came to that part of the text which proved them to be mistaken, they made the application themselves.

### Independent systematic study.

When the last booklet in the story of Ulysses was taken up, there was time for but one lesson with the class, so that results had to be hurried somewhat. The pupils had already stated the questions to be answered and these constituted the aims in reading this section. They were told to read through the entire booklet of eight pages silently, then to make a list of the important subjects in it, to write any questions which they would like to have answered, and any words in place of which they have little reality, or will be eliminated by adjustment in course of experience in teaching the method.

There is a wide field for experiment in connection with problem of teaching pupils how to study independently and tematically, and it is hoped that many of the people most vit concerned, that is, the teachers of classes in the element schools, will take up the matter thoughtfully and earnestly give it a thorough, unbiased trial. By so doing, they can mak valuable contribution to the cause of education.

would like to have other words used. These papers were written by the pupils with no help whatever save in regard to spelling, use of capital letters, and punctuation. Some of the papers are here reported just as they were written.

ROSE.

1. Ulysses awakens.
2. The swineherd gives food to Ulysses.
3. Telemachus goes to the swineherd's house.
4. Ulysses tells Telemachus that he is his beloved father.
5. Ulysses dines with Telemachus, and the swineherd.
6. Telemachus goes to town to see his mother.
7. Telemachus tells Penelope what had happened when he was away.
8. Ulysses goes to the palace as a beggar.
9. Penelope hears of the shameful treatment.
10. Ulysses tells Penelope what he had heard from Ulysses not long ago.
11. The nurse gives Ulysses a bath.
12. The nurse fells (feels) Ulysses scar.
13. Ulysses kills the suitors.
14. Telemachus and Ulysses goes to the house of Laertes.
15. Ulysses reigned over Ithaca as beloved as before.

Why did Ulysses kill the suitors, why did he not send them away?

Why did Ulysses go to town as a beggar, why did he not show himself?

Why didn't Ulysses tell the swineherd he was his master?

Why did Telemachus and Ulysses store the weapons in the inner rooms?

Why don't Ulysses tell Penelope that he was Ulysses instead of telling her that he has fought by Ulysses' side?

Why did Ulysses sleep, why did he not wake up and go to town?

Why did Ulysses go to the house of Laertes?

scrip
revels
threatened
dole

EARL.

1. Ulysses awakes.
2. Ulysses and the swineherd.
3. Ulysses meets Telemachus again.
4. Penelope and Telemachus.
5. Penelope and the beggar.
6. The nurse recognizes Ulysses.
7. Penelope gives a contest.
8. Ulysses tries the bow.
9. The death of the suitors.
10. Ulysses rules over Ithaca again.

Why did Ulysses go to the swineherd?
Why did Ulysses beg for his bread?
Why didn't Ulysses tell Penelope that he was her husband?
Why did Telemachus go to the house of Laertes?

| | | |
|---|---|---|
| procured | treachery | rumor |
| scrip | abusive | adjourned |
| thong | bower | covenant |
| revels | combat | reigned |

Several papers were prepared which were quite equal to Earl's and some might be considered better. The rest would grade in excellence from these down to the following one prepared by a boy who had been in class only two or three days when the exercises was given:

1. When Ulysses wakened from his sleep.
2. He bought from a sheapherd a ragged dirty clock (cloak).
3. He went to visit the swineheard.
4. As she bathed his feet she touched the scar.

This series of lessons showed plainly that pupils in the fourth grade are capable of finding problems for themselves, of organizing the lesson, of asking intelligent questions, of forming sensible hypotheses, of exercising judgment as to the statements made by the author, of mastering formal difficulties for themselves, and, in various ways, of exercising initiative wisely and profitably. It shows, too, that when pupils work in such a way they work with zeal, and accomplish much more than is done

when they must spend time upon useless details and mechanical methods of working.

*Conclusions based upon tests and experiments.*

The fourth grade was selected for these tests because it is usually the lowest grade in the intermediate department of the elementary schools, and it was thought that whatever abilities such pupils possess might reasonably be looked for to at least as great a degree in all of the intermediate and grammar grades. The results of this series of lessons, coupled with the results of the tests in geography given to the sixth and seventh grades, indicate strongly that pupils in the elementary schools in grades including the fourth as well as higher classes, are able not only to employ the factors of logical study, but also that by means of systematic efforts, they can be made to improve in their employment of them. Whether the use of the factors or steps can be made habitual is another problem, as is also the length of time required for such results, and the methods to be employed in securing them. The economy of time and effort which can be accomplished by their use; the effect of their employment upon the so-called dull or stupid pupils; their influence upon schoolroom procedure and discipline—all these problems await solution. One thing is sure, when these factors are recognized by the teacher and used by the class, the centre of gravity, of which Professor Dewey speaks, will no longer lie outside of the child. Growth in right ways of working, in ability to recognize and master problems, and to acquire knowledge will share part of the emphasis now attached almost exclusively to the acquisition of facts.

The use of the factors of study by pupils will bring attending difficulties in the tendency to question unimportant matters, to dwell long on trifles, and, in general, to fail to distinguish between the essential and non-essential. All such difficulties will need facing and solving, just as other problems must be met and solved; but to meet them by refusing all initiative, all freedom, all independence of effort in pupils, is to sacrifice the pupils to the problem. There is no solution in such a procedure. It is believed that when there is a clear understanding of the nature of proper study, and a thoughtful attempt to train pupils in its use, many of the difficulties which at first seem great, will prove to

# APPENDIX

## FIRST SERIES

### Test A, Sixth Grade

Here is a lesson from a book such as you use in class. Do whatever you think you ought to do in studying this lesson thoroughly, and then tell (write down) the different things you have done in studying it. Do not write anything else.

"NORTHERN AFRICA.—The African side of the Mediterranean sea, being so close to Asia and Europe, has long been settled by the white race. Many of the inhabitants are Arabs, who, being believers in Mohammed, still make pilgrimages to Mecca in Arabia, like other followers of that prophet.

"The best known country in this section is Egypt, and CAIRO, its capital, is the largest city in Africa, being about twice the size of New Orleans. ALEXANDRIA is the chief Egyptian port.

"Most of Egypt is a desert country, like Arabia on the one side and the Sahara Desert on the other. The Nile River flows through this desert, and every year the heavy floods from the mountains of Abyssinia and the forest country near the Equator, cause it to rise higher and higher until it overflows its banks. These floods, spreading out over the flood plain and level delta of the Nile, irrigate the land.

"As in other rivers, the water carries with it an abundance of mud, which settles in a thin layer of rich soil upon the flood plain, making it so fertile that excellent crops of cotton, sugar-cane, and grain can be raised after the water is gone. By this means millions of people obtain food, although they live in a desert region.

"On the desert of Sahara few people are able to live. Some parts are sandy plains, while others are rocky and hilly, and in places even mountainous. But here and there, as in Arabia, are oases where water comes from underground, so that grass and date palms are able to grow. Sometimes these oases are so large that villages are built upon them."

## SECOND SERIES

### Test A, Sixth Grade

Here is a lesson from a book such as you use in class. Do whatever you think you ought to do in studying this lesson thoroughly, and then tell (write down) the different things you have done in studying it. Do not write anything else.

6

"When the Puritans settled New England it was very expensive to bring from over the sea the articles that they needed. Nevertheless, at first they imported not only furniture and tools, but even wood for the interior of houses and bricks for the walls, fireplaces, and chimneys. Even now, in some of the older New England buildings, one sees doors and rafters that came from across the ocean many generations ago.

"Very soon, however, the settlers began to make for themselves such articles as shoes, cloth, and lumber. Thus manufacturing began early in this region, and the industry was greatly aided by the water power, caused by the glacier. It was also aided by the many lakes. These serve as reservoirs from which, even during times of drought, a steady supply of water is secured for the falls and rapids.

"Many mills and factories sprang up near the coast, and later in the interior, and thus New England soon became the principal manufacturing section of the whole country. Its many large cities owe their existence chiefly to this industry. Hundreds of articles are made, those composed of cotton, wool, leather, and metal being the most important.

"It may seem strange that this should be the case, since none of these raw materials are extensively produced in New England. But the abundant waterfalls furnished such excellent power that it paid to bring the raw materials there to be manufactured. Therefore, chiefly on account of its water power, manufacturing developed in New England."

## FIRST SERIES

### Test A, Seventh Grade

Here is a lesson from a book such as you use in class. Do whatever you think you ought to do in studying this lesson thoroughly, and then tell (write down) the different things you have done in studying it. Do not write anything else.

"Egypt.—In the movement westward of the people who dwelt along the eastern shores of the Mediterranean and further east in Asia, Egypt became one of the highways of the world, and against its people many destructive wars were waged. As other nations have advanced the Egyptians have steadily lost ground. The famous conqueror, Alexander the Great, overcame them and founded the city of Alexandria; later the Romans made conquest of the territory; and repeatedly since then the country has been invaded, for it has continued to be a highway of trade for three continents. At present Egypt is required to pay annual tribute to Turkey, but she is otherwise practically independent of Turkey; and the ruler, or *Khedive,* is a hereditary monarch. The government of Egypt was so bad that the French and British finally stepped in and took control of the finances of the nation. When the French declined to aid in subduing a rebellion in Egypt, the British alone assumed a large share in the control of Egyptian affairs.

"As a result of British direction there has recently been marked progress in Egypt. Extensive irrigation works have been undertaken,

and the land area for cotton and sugar-cane has thereby been greatly
increased. By means of reservoirs and canals it is further proposed to
reclaim thousands of square miles of desert. A number of railway lines
has also been built, including a part of the proposed line from Cairo to
Cape Town. Outside of the Nile Valley, however, travel still depends
largely upon the use of camels."

## SECOND SERIES.

### Test A, Seventh Grade

Here is a lesson from a book such as you use in class. Do whatever
you think you ought to do in studying this lesson thoroughly, and then
tell (write down) the different things you have done in studying it. Do
not write anything else.

"Climate of Europe.—The direction in which the Highlands extend
is a second cause of great difference between the climates of Europe
and America. In America, where high mountains extend north and
south along the entire western margin of the continent, the warm, damp
westerlies are soon deprived of their moisture. This leaves a vast arid
and semi-arid area in the interior.

"In Europe, on the other hand, where the higher ranges extend nearly
east and west, the mountains do not so seriously interfere with the movement of vapor to the interior. Consequently the west winds surrender
their moisture only very gradually. This accounts for the fact that in
the belt of westerlies, from western Ireland to eastern Russia, there is
rainfall enough for agriculture.

"The east-west direction of the lofty mountains has a marked influence on the climate of those portions of Europe that lie on their north
and south sides. Rising like great walls, the mountains prevent south
winds from bearing northward the heat of the Mediterranean basin; and
they also interfere with the passage of the chilled winds from the north.
We know that Florida, much further south than southern Europe, is
visited by cold waves and accompanying frosts; but mountain barriers
prevent such winds in portions of southern Europe.

"The numerous inland seas are another great factor in influencing
the climate of parts of Europe. * * * It is this influence, added to that
of the mountain barrier, that gives to southern Italy, Greece, France and
Spain such an equable and almost tropical climate."

## FIRST SERIES

### Test C. Sixth Grade

Do not answer this question, but write everything you think
you ought to do in finding the answer to it.

Why is Pittsburg such an important commercial and manufacturing
centre?

## SECOND SERIES

### Test C, Sixth Grade

Do not answer this question, but write everything you think you ought to do in finding the answer to it.

Tobacco used to be grown almost entirely in the Southern States, but now it is grown extensively in the Northern States as well. Why has this change come about?

## FIRST SERIES

### Test C, Seventh Grade

Do not answer this question but write everything you think you ought to do in finding the answer to it.

Why do terrible famines occur in India every few years?

## SECOND SERIES

### Test C, Seventh Grade

Do not answer this question, but write everything you think you ought to do in finding the answer to it.

If you were a voter and a governor was to be elected in your state, how would you decide which of the candidates to vote for?

## FIRST SERIES

### Test E, Sixth Grade

"A swift river rolls stones and sand along its bed and thus wears it deeper. After long ages the bed in which the river flows may be worn down almost to the level of the sea. Its current will be slow and its wearing power very slight.

"Most large rivers flow slowly, because they have already worn their beds down to gentle slopes. The slow current favors the use of boats on rivers.

"While a stream is deepening its bed, the rock waste all over its basin is weathering finer and finer. This waste is always creeping and washing into the valley bottom or into streams that carry it away. Thus the valley grows wider and its side slopes become more gradual. The uplands or hills on either side become smaller and lower, as they slowly waste away.

"In a very long time, even a highland may be worn away to a lowland. Thousands of years are needed for this great work, but the earth is very old, and highland after highland has been worn down.

"Lands whose valleys are not yet widened may be called *young,* even though their streams have been working thousands of years.

"Lands whose valleys are greatly widened, and whose hills or mountains are almost worn away, may be called *old.*

In the middle-aged country, the uplands are deeply and widely cut by valleys. The rainwater runs quickly from the uplands and carries away much land waste. In the old land, most of the upland is worn down and only a few hills remain. In time, even the hills will waste away. Then the streams will become sluggish, but they may be useful as water ways.

"We cannot watch a land grow to old age, for the change is very slow, lasting many hundred thousand years."

## SECOND SERIES

### Test E, Sixth Grade

"Georgia is one of the leading cotton growing states, and exceeds all other states in the yield of peaches. The crops of sweet potatoes, rice, and sugar are also large. The pine forests yield much lumber, and more turpentine and rosin than any other region in the world. There are valuable quarries of marble and granite in the north, Georgia ranking as second state in the production of marble. The fine water power along the Fall line, and the coal and iron mines in the north, give Georgia a high manufacturing rank among the Southern states. The chief manufactures are cotton, lumber, and naval stores.

"*Atlanta,* the capital, was destroyed during the Civil War, but has grown rapidly since, and is one of the greatest commercial cities and railroad centres of the South. It owes its prosperity largely to its location near the southern end of the massive Blue Ridge, and thus where communication is easy with the North and with both the eastern and western groups of Southern railroads. It has cotton mills and many other manufactories.

"*Savannah* was the first place settled in the state. It was taken by the British during the Revolution and was the scene of fighting during the Civil War. It is eighteen miles from the ocean, but has one of the deepest harbors on the Southern coast. The first steamship to cross the Atlantic sailed from this port. Savannah ships much cotton, rice, and lumber, and more naval stores than any other port in the world."

## FIRST AND SECOND SERIES

### Test E, Sixth Grade

Write the answers to these questions, numbering them as the questions are numbered.

1. What is the subject of this lesson?
2. Write a list of the principal topics in it.

3. What do you think is the most important thing in this lesson?
4. What are your reasons for thinking this so important?
5. What other facts do you know about any of these topics?
6. What questions would you ask in regard to anything in this lesson that is not clear to you or that you would like to know more about?

## FIRST SERIES

### TEST E, SEVENTH GRADE

"India is about half as large as the United States, but its population is about four times as great. There are people of various types in all parts of the country, yet they are but little mixed. By far the greatest part of the population. consists of Hindus, a dark-skinned branch of the Aryan people.

"Within the past three centuries the English, French, and Portuguese established trading stations on the coast. The British finally gained control over nearly all the native states, and now govern almost the entire country, although the number of British people in India is quite insignificant in comparison with the dense native population. The King of Great Britain is called the Emperor of India. He appoints a British governor general, or viceroy, who lives in India and governs the country under the direction of the executive branch of the British government in London.

"Most of the people live by agriculture, raising millet and rice for their own use, and various other products for export * * * * *

"Manufacturing industries are being rapidly developed by the Europeans, and cotton, woolen, and jute goods, and paper are made. There are some iron mines in India, and many coal mines, but they are not close together, and there are consequently but few manufactures of iron * * * *

"The British have caused good roads to be constructed in nearly all parts of the country, and have built more than 20,000 miles of railroad. These are the chief means of transportation, for the detritus in the rivers of northern India, and cascades in the rivers of the Deccan interfere with the use of those streams as trade routes."

## SECOND SERIES

### TEST E, SEVENTH GRADE

"We have seen that the people in the various parts of the earth do not all look alike, do not eat the same kinds of food, do not wear the same style of clothing, nor live in the same kinds of houses.

"Near the Kongo river there are black savages living in straw huts, with no books, no lamps, no rifles.

"The Indians in the selvas spend their time in fishing and hunting. They wear but little clothing and use blowguns and bows and arrows.

"On the islands southeast of Asia, brown people live in bamboo huts, and raise rice, coffee, and spices. There the boys make baskets and the girls weave cloth.

"We have read about the Chinese with their long braided hair and their slanting eyes. We have learned that they weave fine silk and pack boxes of tea.

"We know that white people live in our own country and in many other countries. We have seen their books, railroads, ships, workshops, and homes, or pictures of them.

"The people of the earth are divided into five groups, or races. The people of one race differ from those of the other races in color, in size, in the shapes of their skulls, in kinds of hair, in language, and in other respects.

"In some places we shall find that people of two or more races live side by side, but certain lands are known as the home of each race. Thus, America is the home of the Indian, or red-brown race. Most of the brown people are found on islands southeast of Asia. The north and east slopes from the Asian highland are the home of the yellow race. The home of each race is bounded on nearly all sides by oceans, deserts, or lofty highlands. The desert of Sahara lies between lands of the black and the white races. The Himalaya mountains separate homes of yellow and of white people. The land of the Indian is bounded on all sides by the sea."

## FIRST AND SECOND SERIES

### TEST E, SEVENTH GRADE

Write the answers to these questions, numbering them as the questions are numbered.

1. What is the subject of this lesson?
2. Write a list of the principal topics in it.
3. What do you think is the most important thing in this lesson?
4. What are your reasons for thinking this so important?
5. What other facts do you know about any of these topics?
6. What questions would you ask in regard to anything in this lesson that is not clear to you or that you would like to know more about?

## DIRECTIONS FOR THE PRINCIPALS IN REGARD TO CONDUCTING THE TESTS IN GEOGRAPHY

1. In each test, each pupil should write at the top of the first page the following data:

City ...............State .................Date ................
Name of school....................Grade....................
Full name of pupil.......................Age at last birthday
and date of last birthday...........................
Minutes required to write the test..............................

If more than one sheet is required, the pupil should write his name on the extra sheets. He should use ink and write on one side of the sheet only.

2. The tests should be given during the forenoon, and on successive days, test A being given on the first day, test B on the second, etc.

3. The pupils should write these tests without help of *any kind* from *any one.* The results are valueless for the purpose intended unless the work is absolutely the pupils' own.

4. Each child should have as much time as he needs for each test. Children do not work at the same rate of speed and unless each child has the time he needs, the test is not uniform. Begin to count time after the heading is written. Be sure each child indicates it.

5. Results should be sent in from all children present in the class when the test is given. The printed slips should also be collected and returned.

6. Fasten together each set of test papers written by a class, and label it as to grade and test, e.g., Seventh Grade, Test A. When all tests have been given, return the papers to me.

7. If the class is not to be trained, the teacher should not know that there is to be a second series of tests, and if it can be avoided, no teacher should know the nature of the tests before they are given to the class.

8. The pupils must make their own interpretations, do their own spelling, etc. This requirement being uniform will not be a hardship for any particular class, and failure to observe it will vitiate the results.

9. All the printed slips should be returned to me, and no teacher training her class in habits of study should use the contents of the slips for a lesson. She should work with other subject matter and not refer directly to the tests. The classes are to be trained in the habits of study and not coached for a second test.

10. When test A is given, the class should be observed as it works, and notes taken as to what the different pupils do. If a pupil gets one or more books for reference, consults the dictionary, sits and thinks, etc., it should be noted, so that the teacher's notes can be compared with the child's account of what he has done. These notes should be sent with the test papers when they are completed.

11. Test A is the only one in which the pupils may be permitted to consult books, and they are to do that in test A only if they think of it themselves.

12. When test D is given, the pupils are to have first the printed sheet containing the printed matter to be studied. When a child thinks he has completed the study, he is to return this sheet to the teacher and get the slip containing the questions he is to answer. *The slip containing the subject matter must be returned before the questions are given to the pupil.*

13. In test E, the pupils are to have both slips, i.e., subject matter and questions, *at the same time* throughout the test.

Please do not let the teacher talk to her class about the tests. I have tried to include in the directions on the printed slips all that the pupils need to know. For example, when the subject matter for test D is given to the children, the latter ought not to be told that they are to answer questions about the lesson on the slips. The directions say to study the lesson until the pupil thinks he knows it, and that is all he is to know about it until he returns that slip and gets the one containing the questions. If teachers begin talking, there can be no uniformity of procedure in the different classes. Of course the pupils must be told how to write the heading. It is best to write a model of it on the blackboard.

### QUESTIONNAIRE ON OBSERVATIONS OF LESSONS

For the sake of helping to solve some problems in reading, will you please make out for me reports of one or more lessons according to the outline below? The grades should be the fourth, fifth or sixth. The teacher should not know that you are going to make a report. Conditions should be as normal as possible. Report on what teacher does, not on what she knows how to do.

City ................Building ................Grade ................
Date ...........Text-book ...........Name of selection.............

Assignment of lesson

What did the teacher say about

    Difficult words:
    Thought content of selection to be studied:
    Allusions or figures of speech:
    What were pupils to do in preparing the lesson?

In the recitation of this lesson, after it had been studied, what was done in regard to

Difficult words:
Thought Content:
Allusions or figures of speech:
Please report more than one teacher if you have time?

## Teachers' Questionnaire

1. Assuming that memorizing is one of the processes employed in studying, tell how you would memorize a poem or a chapter in the Bible.

2. Many teachers when directing pupils to study, tell them *to think* about the lesson. Enumerate the various things which you think ought to be done in "thinking about a lesson."

3. Is there any thing else which you think ought to be done in studying a lesson?

4. Do you do any of the things named under 1, 2, and 3 more frequently than the others? If so, which are they?

5. When you were a pupil in the Elementary School, were you taught to use any of these steps or processes systematically? If so, which ones?

6. If you have taught in an Elementary School, have you ever trained your pupils there to use any of these steps or processes? If you have, which steps or processes were they?

| CLASS* | Grade | No. of pupils | Average age First test | Average age Second test | Minutes required to write test First test | Minutes required to write test Second test | Read lesson as a whole First Series N. P. | Read lesson as a whole Second Series N. P. | Wrote the facts of the lesson First Series N. P. | Wrote the facts of the lesson Second Series N. P. | Men... First Series N. P. | Prepared questions First Series N. P. | Prepared questions Second Series N. P. | Asked others for help First Series N. P. | Asked others for help Second Series N. P. | Studied words First Series N. P. | Studied words Second Series N. P. |
|---|---|---|---|---|---|---|---|---|---|---|---|---|---|---|---|---|---|
| 1 | 6th | 16 | 12.1 | 12.2 | 23 | 10 | *2 12.5* 4 25. | 43.8 | 7 43.8 | | | *1 6.3* | | *1 6.3* | | *1 6.3* | |
| 2 | 5th & 6th | 18 | 12. | 12.2 | 16 | 6 | *2 11.1* 11 61.1 | 1 5.6 | | 5 27. | | | | | | *1 5.6* 3 16.7 | 4 22.2 |
| 3 | 6A | 35 | 11.8 | 12. | 5 | 17 | 15 42.9 | 4.3 | | 14 40. | 1 2.9 | | 5 14.3 | | | 3 8.6 | 15 42.9 |
| 4 | 6B | 33 | 11.8 | 12. | 8 | 10 | *3 9.1* 13 39.4 | 36.4 | 6 18.2 | 12 36. | 2 6.1 | | 2 6.1 | | | 3 9.1 | |
| 5 | 6th | 9 | 11.7 | 12. | 29 | 55 | 6 66.7 | | | 5 55. | | | | | | | 9 100. |
| Totals | | 111 | 11.9 | 12.1 | 16 | 20 | *7 6.3* 49 44.1 | 22.5 | 13 11.7 | 36 32. | *1 .9* 3 2.7 | | 7 6.3 | *1 .9* | | *2 1.8* 9 8.1 | 28 25.2 |
| 6 | 6B¹ | 38 | 12.6 | 12.8 | 25 | 22 | 8 21. | 6.3 | 12 31.6 | 4 10. | 3 7.9 | | 10 26.3 | 1 2.6 | *1 2.6* | | *1 .26* |
| 7 | 6B² | 31 | 12.6 | 12.9 | 27 | 15 | *1 3.2* 5 16.1 | 8.7 | 8 25.8 | 2 6.6 | 2 6.5 4 12.9 | | 3 9.7 4 12.9 | 2 6.5 | *1 3.2* | 2 6.5 | |
| 8 | 6B³ | 37 | 12.5 | 12.8 | 42 | 18 | *1 2.7* 17 45.9 | 43.2 | 2 5.4 | 11 29. | 7 18.9 8 22.9 | | 6 16.2 15 42.9 | 2 5.4 2 5.7 | *1 2.7* | 13 35.1 *1 2.9* | 3 8.1 2 5.7 |
| 9 | 6A² | 35 | | | | | *9 25.7* 1 2.9 | 5.7 | 3 8.6 | 10 28. 1 2.4 | | | 13 37.1 | | | 2 5.7 | |
| 10 | 6B¹ | 38 | | | | | *1 2.6* 19 50. | 13.2 | 5 13.2 | 16 42. | 5 13.2 | | 10 26.8 2 6.5 | 1 2.6 | | 2 5.3 | |
| 11 | 6B² | 31 | | | | | 7 22.6 | 9.4 | 5 16.1 | 2 6.7 3 7.5 | 2 6.5 | | 3 9.7 2 5. | | *1 2.5* | 13 41.9 1 2.5 | *1 3.2* 10 32.2 5 12.5 |
| 12 | 6B¹ | 40 | 12.8 | 13. | 23 | 20 | *5 12.5* 14 35. | 55. | 8 20. | 5 12.5 | 2 5. | | 4 10. | | | | 7 17.5 |
| 13 | 6B² | 38 | 12.7 | 12.9 | 19 | 11 | *1 2.6* 3 7.9 | 71.1 | 6 15.8 | 1 2.2 1 2.3 | 2 5.3 | | 1 2.6 2 4.6 | | | 1 2.6 | 4 10.5 |
| 14 | 6B³ | 43 | 13. | 13.1 | 29 | 29 | *2 4.6* 11 25.6 | 58.1 | 10 23.3 2 4.6 | 6 14. 3 6.2 | 3 7. 1 2.2 | | 2 4.6 5 10.9 | | | 1 2.3 | 3 7. 1 2.2 |
| 15 | 6A¹ | 46 | 12. | 12.2 | 19 | 11 | *1 2.2* 7 15.2 2 4.3 | 87. | 16 34.8 1 2.1 | 7 15.3 3 6.4 | 1 2.2 1 2.1 | | 10 21.7 | 1 2.2 1 2.1 | 1 2.1 | *1 2.1* 2 4.3 | 3 6.4 3 8.3 |
| 16 | 6A² | 47 | 11.9 | 12.3 | 22 | 12 | 23 48.9 2 5.5 | 34. | 2 4.3 1 2.8 | 18 38. 1 2.3 | | | 4 8.5 | | 1 2.8 | | 1 2.8 |
| 17 | 6A³ | 36 | 14. | 14.2 | 19 | 17 | 5 13.9 2 9.5 | 55.5 | 9 25. 2 9.5 | 2 5.7 2 9.8 | | | 2 5.5 | | | | |
| 18 | 6th | 21 | 12.3 | 12.5 | 10 | 4 | 3 14.3 2 8. | 66.7 | 3 14.3 | 2 9.3 2 8. | | | 2 9.5 | | 1 4. | | |
| 19 | 6th | 25 | 12. | 12.3 | 37 | 15 | 2 8. 2 6.1 | 76. | 7 28. | 2 8. 2 6. | | | 3 12. | | 1 3. | 1 4. 1 3. | 1 4. 3 9.1 |
| 20 | 6th | 33 | 12.3 | 12.3 | 13 | 8 | 10 30.3 | 27.2 | 2 6.1 | 8 24. | | | 6 18.2 | 2 6.1 | | | 1 3. |
| Totals | | 539 | 12.6 | 12.8 | 24 | 14 | *31 5.8* 135 25. | 9.4 | *8 1.5* 98 18.2 | *31 5.8* 87 16.4 | 12 2.2 29 5.4 | | 33 6.1 80 14.8 | 4 .7 9 1.7 | 8 1.5 | *4 .7* 37 6.9 | *16 3* 33 6.1 |
| 21 | 7th | 12 | 12.6 | 12.7 | 32 | 28 | 3 25. | 16.7 | 2 16.7 | 2 16.7 1 7.7 | 2 16.7 | | | | *1 3.3* | *1 3.3* 3 23.1 | 1 7.7 |
| 22 | 7th | 13 | 12.4 | 12.8 | 13 | 6 | *1 7.7* 11 85.4 | 10. | | 10 76. | | | 1 7.7 | | | 5 38.5 | 2 15.4 |
| 23 | 7th | 35 | 12.6 | 12.8 | 23 | 8 | 26 74.3 | 2.9 | 1 2.9 | 25 71. | 6 17.1 | | | | 1 4. | *1 2.9* 10 28.6 | 13 37.1 |
| 24 | 7th | 25 | 13.4 | 13.6 | 25 | 11 | *1 4.* 17 68. | 8. | | 10 40. | | | | 1 4. | | 2 8. 7 28. | |
| Totals | | 85 | 12.8 | 13. | 23 | 13 | *2 2.4* 57 67.1 | 5.9 | 3 3.5 | *1 1.2* 47 55.8 | 8 9.4 | | 1 1.2 | 2 2.4 | | *6 7.1* 22 25.9 | *2 2.4* 15 17.6 |
| 25 | 7th | 35 | 13.1 | 13.5 | | | *6 17.1* 15 42.9 | 9.9 | | 5 14. 11 31.9 | 3 8.6 | | | | | *1 2.9* | |
| 26 | 7th | 19 | 13.3 | 13.5 | 21 | 10 | 7 36.8 | 1.6 | 1 5.3 | 1 5. 3 15.3 2 7.7 | 4 21.1 | | 2 7.7 | | 1 3.8 | 5 26.3 1 3.8 | 1 3.8 |
| 27 | 7th | 26 | 12.3 | 12.4 | 11 | 7 | *1 3.8* 14 53.9 | 0.8 | 1 3.8 | 10 38.7 8 26.3 | | | 1 3.3 | 3 10. | 6 20. | 2 7.7 9 30. | 2 6.7 |
| 28 | 7th | 30 | 12.4 | 12.5 | 27 | 26 | *4 13.3* 2 6.7 | 6.7 | 1. 3.3 | 3 10. | 9 30. | | 7 23.3 | | | 2 6.7 | |
| Totals | | 110 | 12.8 | 13. | 20 | 14 | *11 10.* 38 34.5 | 8. 9 | 3 2.7 | *16 14.5* 27 24.6 | 1 .9 16 14.5 | | 2 1.8 7 6.4 | 3 2.7 | 7 6.4 | *11 10.* 4 3.6 | *3 2.7* 5 4.5 |
| Totals | | 845 | | | | | *51 6.* 279 33. | 6. | *8 .9* 117 13.8 | *49 5.9* 197 23.8 | 14 1.7 56 6.6 | | 36 4.3 94 11.1 | 10 1.2 9 1. | 15 1.8 | *23 2.7* 72 8.5 | *21 2.5* 81 9.6 |

* Classes 1–5 and 21–24 were tra... ...udying the lesson.

|  |  |  | Not Clear | Inadequate | | Adequate | | W |
| CLASS* | Grade | No. of Pupils | Second Series | First Series | Second Series | First Series | Second Series | First Series |
|  |  |  | N. P. | N. P. | N. P. | N. P. | N. P. | N. P. |
|---|---|---|---|---|---|---|---|---|
| 1....... | 6th | 7 | 4 26.7 | 6 40. | 6 40. | 1 6.7 | 4 26.7 | ..... |
| 2....... | 6th |  | 2 10. | 5 55. | 14 70. | 8 40. | 4 20. | ..... |
| 3....... | 6A | 4 | 18 51.1 | 10 28.6 | 2 5.7 | 7 20. | 15 42.9 | ..... |
| 4....... | 6B |  | 4 13.3 | 8 26.7 | 6 20. | 9 30. | 18 60. | 1 3.3 |
| 5....... | 6th | 3 | 4 44.4 | ..... | ..... | ..... | 5 55.5 | ..... |
| Totals... |  | 16 | 32 29.4 | 29 26.6 | 28 25.7 | 25 22.9 | 46 42.2 | 1 0.9 10 |
| 6....... | 6B¹ | 1 | 5 12.8 | 6 15.4 | 20 51.3 | 4 10.3 | 5 12.8 | ..... 1 |
| 7....... | 6B² | 5 | 5 14.7 | 8 23.5 | 11 32.4 | 5 14.7 | 13 38.2 | 2 5.9 1 |
| 8....... | 6B³ | 7 | 6 16.2 | 5 13.5 | 10 27. | 14 37.8 | 17 45.9 | 1 |
| 9....... | 6A² | 2 | 9 26.5 | 8 23.5 | 13 38.2 | 13 38.2 | 11 32.4 | 3 |
| 10....... | 6B¹ | 6 | 11 32.4 | 9 26.5 | 16 47.1 | 15 44.1 | 5 14.7 | 1 |
| 11....... | 6B² | 3 | 11 36.7 | 8 26.7 | 12 40. | 8 26.7 | 5 16.7 | 1 3.3 |
| 12....... | 6B¹ | 1 | 5 12.2 | 12 29.3 | 13 31.7 | 10 24.4 | 22 53.7 | 1 2.4 1 |
| 13....... | 6B² | 3 | 10 27. | 9 24.3 | 5 13.5 | 12 32.4 | 21 56.8 | 1 |
| 14....... | 6B³ | 3 | 8 18.2 | 20 45.5 | 23 52.3 | 6 13.6 | 12 27.3 | 2 4.5 |
| 15....... | 6A¹ |  | 7 16.3 | 11 25.6 | 17 39.5 | 6 14. | 9 20.9 | 1 |
| 16....... | 6A² |  | 13 28.3 | 18 39.1 | 19 41.3 | 20 43.5 | 11 23.9 | 2 |
| 17....... | 6A³ | 4 | 9 23.7 | 2 5.3 | 10 26.3 | 13 34.2 | 14 36.8 | 1 2.6 1 |
| 18....... | 6A | 4 | 13 56.5 | 1 4.4 | 1 4.4 | 2 8.7 | 6 26.1 | 2 |
| 19....... | 6A |  | 6 20. | 2 6.7 | 6 20. | 7 23.3 | 16 53.3 | 1 3.3 |
| 20....... | 6A | 4 | 12 36.4 | 2 6.1 | 4 12.1 | 7 21.2 | 13 39.4 | 3 9.1 2 6 |
| 21....... | 6A | 1 | 8 21.6 | 4 10.8 | 13 35.1 | 16 43.2 | 13 35.1 | 2 5 |
| Totals... |  | 5 9 | 138 23.8 | 125 21.6 | 193 33.3 | 158 27.2 | 193 33.3 | 11 1.9 16 2. |
| 22....... | 7th | 4 | ..... | 2 15.4 | 7 53.8 | 11 84.6 | 4 15.4 | ..... 3 23. |
| 23....... | 7th |  | 5 41.7 | 5 41.7 | 4 33.3 | 1 8.3 | 3 25. | 1 8.3 3 25. |
| 24....... | 7th | 9 | 17 60.7 | 6 21.4 | 8 28.6 | 17 60.7 | 2 7.1 | 5 17.9 12 42.9 |
| 25....... | 7th | 8 | 12 41.4 | 11 37.9 | 10 34.5 | 11 37.9 | 6 20.7 | 1 3.5 3 10.3 |
| Totals... |  | 1 | 34 41.5 | 24 29.3 | 29 35.4 | 40 48.8 | 15 18.3 | 7 8.5 21 25.6 |
| 26....... | 7th | 9 | 10 31.3 | 9 28.1 | 12 37.5 | 15 46.9 | 10 31.3 | 1 3.1 5 15.6 |
| 27....... | 7th | 13 | 4 23.5 | 4 23.5 | 5 29.4 | 6 35.3 | 8 47.1 | ..... 2 11.8 |
| 28....... | 7th | 7 | 6 20. | 14 46.7 | 10 33.3 | 8 26.7 | 14 46.7 | 3 10. 11 36.7 |
| 29....... | 7th | 3 | 9 30. | 4 13.3 | 5 16.7 | 24 80. | 16 53.3 | 1 3.3 11 36.7 |
| Totals... |  | 104 | 29 26.6 | 31 28.4 | 32 29.4 | 53 48.6 | 48 44. | 5 4.6 29 26.6 |
| Totals.... |  | 88 1 | 233 26.5 | 209 23.8 | 282 32. | 276 31.4 | 302 34.3 | 24 2.7 76 8.6 |

* Cl

# TABLE III

numbers are placed in one space, the lower one indicates the number of cases, the upper one, the one in
s, represents the per cent of cases.

TABLE V

The Nature of

**TABLE VI**

| CLASS | Number in class | Get idea of lesson as a whole (N.P.) | Solve problems; form and answer questions (N.P.) | Find the important points (N. P.) | Group related ideas (N.) | Supplement the text (N.) | Make experiments; observe, investigate (N. P.) | Discuss (N. P.) | Compare (N. P. N.) | Understand meaning (N. P.) | Visualize (N. P.) | Find illustrations (N.) | Review; summarize (N.) | Give oral or written expression (N.) | Memorize (N.) | Apply knowledge (N P.) | Drill to form habits (N. P.) | Arouse interest (N. P.) | Concentrate attention (N. P.) | Apperceive (N. P. N.) | Correlate (N.) | Reason (N. P. P.) | Study words (N. P. P.) | Preserve the individuality (N. P. N. P.) |
|---|---|---|---|---|---|---|---|---|---|---|---|---|---|---|---|---|---|---|---|---|---|---|---|---|
| 1 | 34 | | 3 8.8 | 9 26.5 | 3 8.8 | 5 14.7 | 7 20.6 | 2 5.9 | 2 5.9 | 2 5.9 | 4 15.4 | | 1 2.9 | 7 20.6 | 3 8.8 | 7 20.6 | | 2 5.9 | 2.9 | 3 8.8 | 3 8.8 | 1 2.9 | 3 13.8 | .8 |
| 2 | 26 | | 8.8 | 5 19.2 | 3 11.5 | 4 15.4 | 1 3.8 | 2 7.7 | | 3 8.3 | 4 15.4 | 4 15.4 | 7.7 | 9 34.6 | 3 11.5 | 7 20.6 | | 1 4.2 | 8.3 | 2 6.3 | 2 8.3 | | 14.2 | 13.8 |
| 3 | 24 | 14.2 | 1 | 3 12.5 | 3 12.5 | 2 8.3 | | | 1 6.3 | 8.3 | 1 6.3 | 1 5.4 | 4.2 | 6 25. | 1 6.3 | 8 33.3 | 4 14.2 | 4.2 | 8. | 2.9 | 6.3 | 4 16.3 | 14.2 | 14.2 |
| 4 | 16 | 1 6.3 | | 2 12.5 | 4 11.4 | 2 12.5 | 2 12.9 | 6.3 | | 5 14.3 | | | | 2 12.5 | 4 6.3 | 2 12.5 | 1 2.9 | 2.9 | 5.7 | 2 5.7 | 1 6.3 | 1 6.3 | | 14.2 |
| 5 | 35 | 1 2.9 | 2.9 5.7 | 7 20. | 4 11.4 | 5 5.7 | 1 12.9 | | | | 1 6.3 | | 2.9 | 6 17.1 | 4 11.4 | 2 12. | 1 2.9 | 9 | 5.7 | 2 2.9 | 2 9.2 | 6.3 | 2.9 | 16.3 |
| 6 | 30 | | | 5 16.7 | 3 3.3 | 2 6.7 | 1 13.3 | | | | 1 6.3 | | 3 10. | 3 10. | 6 20. | 4 11.4 | 2 2.9 | 3 10. | 4 13.3 | 3 3.3 | 3 3.3 | 1 6.3 | 3 10. | |
| Totals & per cents | 165 | 3 1.8 | 1.86 3.6 | 31 18.8 | 8.5 14 | 10.3 17 | 10 6.1 | 15 3. | 3 1.8 | 11 6.7 | 5 3. | 4 2.48 | 4.8 | 33 20. | 18 10.9 | 25 15.2 | 1.27 | 4.29 | 5.54 | 2.47 | 4.23 | 1.86 | 3.63 1.8 | 1.8 |

## TABLE VII

| CLASS | Number in class | Recognize the problem; determine the aim N. | P. | Find the important points N. | P. | Group related ideas N. | P. | Formulate questions N. | P. | Get the logical connections N. | P. | Use references N. | P. | Visualize; imagine N. | P. | Compare N. | P. | Review; summarize N. | P. | Give oral or written expression N. | P. | Apply knowledge N. | P. | Think; reason; understand the lesson N. | P. | Perceive N. | P. | Appreceive N. | P. | Memorize N. | P. | Arouse, interest N. | P. | Concentrate attention N. | P. | Other answers N. | P. |
|---|---|---|---|---|---|---|---|---|---|---|---|---|---|---|---|---|---|---|---|---|---|---|---|---|---|---|---|---|---|---|---|---|---|---|---|---|---|
| 1 | 34 | 1 | 2.9 | 4 | 11.8 | 8 | 23.5 | 1 | 2.9 | . | . | 2 | 5.9 | 1 | 2.9 | 4 | 11.8 | 2 | 5.9 | 2 | 5.9 | 3 | 8.8 | 11 | 32.4 | 2 | 5.9 | 1 | 2.9 | 9 | 26.5 | 2 | 5.9 | 3 | 8.8 | . | . |
| 2 | 26 | . | . | 7 | 26.9 | 7 | 26.9 | 2 | 7.7 | 1 | 3.8 | . | . | 3 | 11.5 | 1 | 3.8 | 1 | 3.8 | 1 | 3.8 | 2 | 7. | 1 | 3.8 | . | . | . | . | 5 | 19.2 | . | . | 1 | 8.8 | . | . |
| 3 | 24 | . | . | 4 | 16.7 | 3 | 12.5 | . | . | . | . | 1 | 4.2 | . | . | 2 | 8.3 | . | . | 2 | 8.3 | 1 | 4.2 | 6 | 25. | . | . | 1 | 4.2 | 5 | 20.8 | . | . | 3 | 12.5 | 3 | 11.5 |
| 4 | 16 | 1 | 2.9 | 3 | 18.8 | . | . | 2 | 5.7 | . | . | . | . | 3 | 8.6 | 1 | 6.3 | . | . | 1 | 6.3 | 2 | 12.5 | 3 | 18.8 | . | . | 3 | 18.8 | 5 | 31.3 | . | . | . | . | . | . |
| 5 | 35 | . | . | 12 | 34.3 | 7 | 20. | . | . | 1 | 3.3 | . | . | . | . | . | . | 1 | 2.9 | 4 | 11.4 | 2 | 5.7 | 9 | 25.7 | . | . | 2 | 5.7 | 12 | 34. | . | . | 1 | 2.9 | 1 | 6.3 |
| 6 | 30 | . | . | 5 | 16.7 | . | . | . | . | . | . | . | . | . | . | . | . | 4 | 13.3 | 1 | 3.3 | 1 | 3.3 | 4 | 13.3 | . | . | 2 | 6.7 | 4 | 13.3 | . | . | 2 | 6.7 | . | . |
| Totals and per cents | 165 | 2 | 1.2 | 35 | 21.2 | 25 | 15.2 | 5 | 3. | 2 | 1.2 | 3 | 1.8 | 7 | 4.2 | 8 | 4.8 | 8 | 4.8 | 11 | 6.7 | 11 | 6.7 | 34 | 20.6 | 2 | 1.2 | 9 | 5.5 | 40 | 24.2 | 2 | 1.2 | 10 | 6.1 | 4 | 2.4 |

**TABLE VIII**

| CLASS | Number in class | Read the text N. | Read the text P. | Find the main thoughts N. | Find the main thoughts P. | Understand the thought N. | Understand the thought P. | Verify the author's statements N. | Verify the author's statements P. | Reason N. | Reason P. | Memorize N. | Memorize P. | Apply knowledge N. | Apply knowledge P. | Study the new words N. | Study the new words P. | Concentrate attention N. | Concentrate attention P. | Do not remember—have forgotten N. | Do not remember—have forgotten P. | Were not taught to study N. | Were not taught to study P. | Answer not relevant N. | Answer not relevant P. | Other answers N. | Other answers P. |
|---|---|---|---|---|---|---|---|---|---|---|---|---|---|---|---|---|---|---|---|---|---|---|---|---|---|---|---|
| 1 | 34 | | | 1 | 2.9 | 2 | 5.9 | | | 1 | 2.9 | 4 | 11.8 | | | 1 | 2.9 | 2 | 5.9 | 8 | 23.5 | 15 | 44.1 | 4 | 11.8 | | |
| 2 | 26 | | | | | 1 | 3.8 | | | | | 3 | 11.5 | 1 | 3.8 | | | | | 5 | 19.2 | 15 | 57.7 | 1 | 3.8 | 1 | 3.8 |
| 3 | 24 | | | 1 | 4.2 | 1 | 4.2 | 2 | 8.3 | | | 7 | 29.2 | 1 | 4.2 | 1 | 4.2 | 1 | 4.2 | 3 | 12.5 | 11 | 45.8 | 2 | 8.3 | 2 | 8.3 |
| 4 | 16 | 2 | 12.5 | | | | | | | | | 4 | 25. | | | | | | | 1 | 6.3 | 9 | 56.3 | 1 | 6.3 | | |
| 5 | 35 | | | 1 | 2.9 | 3 | 8.6 | | | | | 11 | 31.4 | | | | | | | 2 | 5.7 | 16 | 45.7 | | | 2 | 5.7 |
| 6 | 30 | 3 | 10. | 4 | 13.3 | 4 | 13.3 | 1 | 3.3 | 1 | 3.3 | 5 | 16.7 | 1 | 3.3 | | | 1 | 3.3 | 2 | 6.7 | 10 | 33.3 | 2 | 6.7 | 2 | 6.7 |
| Totals and per cents | 165 | 5 | 3. | 7 | 4.2 | 11 | 6.7 | 3 | 1.8 | 2 | 1.2 | 34 | 20.6 | 3 | 1.8 | 2 | 1.2 | 4 | 2.4 | 21 | 12.7 | 76 | 46.1 | 10 | 6.1 | 7 | 4.2 |

## TABLE IX

| CLASS | Number in class | Get idea of whole lesson | Find the subject, the problem | Find the principal points | Group related ideas | Formulate questions | Supplement the text | Compare | Verify the author's statements | Visualize; imagine | Recall related ideas | Form independent judgments | Determine when the question is answered | Review or summarize | Drill |
|---|---|---|---|---|---|---|---|---|---|---|---|---|---|---|---|
| | | N. P. | N. P. | N. P. | N. P. | N.P. | N. P. | N. P. | N.P. | N. P. | N. P. | N. P. | N. P. | N. P. | N. P. |
| 1........ | 34 | 4 11.8 | ..... | 5 14.7 | 8 23.5 | ..... | 3 8.8 | 7 20.6 | 2 5.9 | 2 5.9 | 4 11.8 | 3 8.8 | 1 2.9 | 2 5.9 | 2 5.9 |
| 2........ | 26 | 1 3.8 | ..... | 3 11.5 | 5 19.2 | 1 3.8 | 1 3.8 | 1 3.8 | ..... | 4 15.4 | | | | | |
| 3........ | 24 | 1 4.2 | ..... | 4 16.7 | 8 33.3 | .... | 1 4.2 | 3 12.5 | 2 8.3 | ...... | | | | 2 8.3 | 2 8.3 |
| 4........ | 16 | 2 12.5 | ..... | 2 12.5 | 4 25. | 1 6.3 | 2 12.5 | 2 12.5 | ..... | | | | | | 1 6.3 |
| 5........ | 35 | ...... | 3 8.6 | 3 8.6 | 2 5.7 | 3 8.6 | 1 2.9 | 1 2.9 | 1 2.9 | 1 2.9 | | | | 1 2.9 | ..... |
| 6........ | 30 | 6 20. | ..... | 5 16.7 | 3 10. | 1 3.3 | 1 3.3 | 1 3.3 | ..... | 4 13.3 | | | | 1 3.3 | |
| Totals.. | 165 | 14 8.5 | 3 1.8 | 22 13.3 | 30 18.2 | 6 3.6 | 9 5.5 | 15 9.1 | 4 2.4 | 11 6.7 | 4 2.4 | 3 1.8 | 1 .6 | 6 3.6 | 5 3. |

## TABLE IX—*Continued*

| Memorize | | Give oral or written expression | | Apply knowledge | | Discuss | | Reason; understand thought | | Study new words or phrases | | Arouse interest | | Concentrate attention | | Perceive | | Apperceive | | Correlate | | Answer not relevant | | Have not taught pupils to study systematically | | Have not taug... elementary | |
|---|---|---|---|---|---|---|---|---|---|---|---|---|---|---|---|---|---|---|---|---|---|---|---|---|---|---|---|
| N. | P. | N. | P. | N. | P. | N. | P. | N. | P. | N. | P. | N. | P. | N. | P. | N. | P. | N. | P. | N. | P. | N. | P. | N. | P. | N. | P. |
| 11 | 32.4 | 2 | 5.9 | 3 | 8.8 | 2 | 5.9 | 11 | 32.4 | 2 | 5.9 | 2 | 5.9 | 7 | 20.6 | 5 | 14.7 | | | | | 6 | 17.6 | | | 2 | 5.9 |
| 6 | 23.1 | 2 | 7.7 | 3 | 11.5 | | | 3 | 11.5 | 1 | 3.8 | | | 2 | 7.7 | | | | | | | 3 | 11.5 | 3 | 11.5 | 8 | 30.8 |
| 7 | 29.2 | | | | | | | 15 | 62.5 | | | | | 3 | 12.5 | | | | | | | 2 | 8.3 | 2 | 8.3 | 4 | 16.7 |
| 8 | 50. | 1 | 6.3 | 4 | 25 | 1 | 6.3 | 5 | 31.3 | | | | | 1 | 6.3 | | | | | | | 3 | 18.8 | | | 1 | 6.3 |
| 9 | 25.7 | 4 | 11.4 | 2 | 5.7 | | | 10 | 28.6 | 3 | 8.6 | 2 | 5.7 | 3 | 8.6 | 1 | 2.9 | 4 | 11.4 | 3 | 8.6 | | | 5 | 14.3 | 2 | 5.7 |
| 9 | 30. | 1 | 3.3 | | | | | 12 | 40. | 3 | 10. | 1 | 3.3 | 4 | 13.3 | | | 1 | 3.3 | | | 1 | 3.3 | 1 | 3.3 | 9 | 30. |
| 50 | 30.3 | 10 | 6.1 | 12 | 7.3 | 3 | 1.8 | 56 | 33.9 | 9 | 5.5 | 5 | 3. | 20 | 12.1 | 6 | 3.6 | 5 | 3. | 3 | 1.8 | 15 | 9.1 | 11 | 6.7 | 26 | 15.8 |